JEREMIAH
Elizabeth Achtemeier

KNOX PREACHING GUIDES
John H. Hayes, Editor

John Knox Press
ATLANTA

Library of Congress Cataloging-in-Publication Data

Achtemeier, Elizabeth Rice, 1926–
 Jeremiah.

 (Knox preaching guides)
 Bibliography: p.
 1. Bible. O.T. Jeremiah—Commentaries. 2. Bible.
O.T. Jeremiah—Homiletical use. I. Title. II. Series.
BS1525.3.A24 1987   224'.207   86-45402
ISBN 0-8042-3222-9

© copyright John Knox Press 1987
10 9 8 7 6 5 4 3 2 1
Printed in the United States of America
John Knox Press
Atlanta, Georgia 30365

Contents

[Sequential Guide to Passages on next page]

Sequential Guide to Jeremiah Passages

JEREMIAH

Introduction

Few books are more pivotal in biblical theology than the book of Jeremiah. This is true, first, because of its historical setting. Jeremiah's ministry spanned the years of Judah's life from 626 to about 584 B.C. and in those decades, great sea changes took place in the history of the ancient Near East. The Assyrian Empire, which had dominated the Fertile Crescent for a century, fell, and the Neo-Babylonian empire took its place, to hold power for almost another one hundred years. Judah, including Benjamin, the sole survivors among the twelve tribes of Israel, succumbed to Babylonian might and lost their land, their temple, and their kingship, ending the existence of the nation Israel as a political entity. From 587 B.C. on, the Jews would exist as a religious community, except for a brief time under the rule of the Maccabees and finally, from A.D. 1948 on, when the modern Israeli nation was established. It was given to the prophet Jeremiah to interpret such cataclysmic history.

Second, the book of Jeremiah is pivotal for the Judaic-Christian theology of the Bible because it testifies to decisive changes in God's actions and attitudes toward his chosen people. The history of Israel from the time of her deliverance out of bondage in Egypt to the time of the sweeping Deuteronomic reform of her religious life in 622/621 B.C. is a history primarily characterized by God's struggle with his people's sinful rebellion against his rule. Israel constantly backslides, continually strikes out on her own, repeatedly forgets her God and ignores his love and guidance of her life. And through it all God promises and judges, warns and forgives, protests and struggles and grieves. But finally, through the words of Jeremiah, God utters, "Enough!" "I hate her," he declares and breaks out in war against his own people, until her national life is destroyed and only her remnant left among the nations. In Jeremiah's book, God takes decisive, final action against Israel's sin, and it is not until he declares through Second Isaiah that "her warfare is ended" that the sin's punishment is completed.

In the same vein, however, it is also in this record of the prophecies of Jeremiah that God solves the problem of his people's sin—of how to make a faithful people out of such faithless rebels. Because Judah's heart is uncircumcised and her sin written with a point of diamond upon it, God decides that he will change the hearts of his people, erasing their sin and writing his words on their hearts instead, in an interior covenant. And it is this decision that the Lord effects through all of the rest of biblical history, finally shining in our hearts to give the knowledge of God in the face of Jesus Christ. Thus the book of Jeremiah is the crucial bridge to the NT and finds the beginning of its fulfillment in that upper room, when Jesus of Nazareth gives the cup of the new covenant to his disciples. No book leads more surely into the theology of Paul and of the Gospels than does this prophetic work.

To be sure, the book is not easy to read, much less to preach. It divides itself into five broad sections. Chapters 1–25 contain most of the poetic oracles of the prophet to his own people and were apparently first collected together by 605 B.C. (see the account in Jer 36), but they are now interspersed with prose accounts and with later materials. Within these chapters, there are also several small collections, for example 21:11–23:8 "to the house of the king of Judah" or 23:9–40 "concerning the prophets." Chapters 26–29, 32–45 form an historical biography of the prophet, intended to give the occasions for his memorable words. These chapters have most frequently been attributed to Jeremiah's scribe Baruch (see 36:4; 45:1–5). Chapters 30–31 again are made up of poetic oracles and are often named "The Little Book of Comfort."

Some of these oracles date from the prophet's early career, some from his late ministry, and some apparently do not come from Jeremiah at all. Chapters 46–51 contain both poetic and prose oracles against various foreign nations and, with a few exceptions, are generally considered not to come from Jeremiah. Chapter 52 is an historical appendix, largely parallel to 2 Kings 24:18–25:30.

Jeremiah's poetic oracles are some of the finest to be found in the OT and have left their mark upon the imagination and literature of every age. His portrayal of Rachel:

> "A voice is heard in Ramah,
> lamentation and bitter weeping.
> Rachel is weeping for her children . . .
> because they are not" (31:15).

His search of the distant horizon from his northern home in Anathoth for some healing for his people:

> Is there no balm in Gilead?
> Is there no physician there (8:22)?

His shrewd observations of the natural world:

> "The wild asses stand on the bare heights,
> they pant for air like jackals;
> their eyes fail
> because there is no vegetation" (14:6).

His use of poetic metaphors for Israel's wandering ways:

> "Look at your way in the valley;
> know what you have done—
> a restive young camel interlacing her tracks,
> a wild ass used to the wilderness,
> in her heat sniffing the wind!
> Who can restrain her lust?" (2:23–24).

Such passages attest to the rhetorical skill, the imagination, and the sensitivity of this prophetic poet.

And yet the reader of Jeremiah also frequently comes across prose passages replete with stereotyped phrases, superscriptions, dates, and a constant concern with apostasy and calls to repentance that remind of nothing so much as the repetitious accounts in the books of Kings or of the theology of the book of Deuteronomy. Jeremiah is shot through with Deuteronomic language and thought that seem impossible to connect with the skilled poet of the oracles. No problem has given students of Jeremiah more trouble, and the relation of Jeremiah to the Deuteronomic reform under King Josiah has been a perennial subject of scholarly debate. A position is briefly discussed with regard to the matter in this volume. But for purposes of introduction, suffice it to say that the Deuteronomic-like prose passages should be read as true to the thought of the prophet.

Given all that, the question remains, How can one preach from Jeremiah, especially considering the special problems that it presents to the homiletician? First, the material in the book, as in so many prophetic books, is not in chronological order. Chapter 1 immediately raises the difficulty, for it places side by side with the original call of the prophet, two visions probably to be dated at least seventeen years later. Such juxtapositions of variously dated material continue throughout the work. This means that each passage in the book must be isolated and set in its own proper historical context, which in turn implies that the preacher must be familiar with the history of the ancient Near East. This preaching guide tries to help with the problem, but it is also recommended that the preacher familiarize himself or herself with the situation of Judah in its final century by reading a volume like John Bright's *A History of Israel*. To be sure, the preacher should also ask what the final redactors of Jeremiah were saying theologically by ordering the material as they did. Nevertheless, Jeremiah makes the most sense by setting each passage in its specific time and place.

Second among the problems presented to the homiletician by Jeremiah is the fact that so many of his oracles announce God's judgment and that in the form of God's holy war against his own people. Such pronouncements are not received kindly by an age such as ours. Modern Americans do not believe in the judgment of God, and they do not like the terminology of warfare—who sings "Onward Christian Soldiers" anymore? Thus there is an inbuilt prejudice existing in any average congregation against Jeremiah's words at first hearing, a prejudice that the lectionary tries to skirt by using mostly hopeful passages from the book that may be interpreted as fulfilled in Christ. But the preacher has a rare opportunity, using Jeremiah, to enlarge the congregation's understanding of the biblical God who is always at the same time Judge and Savior, Warrior and Healer, Destroyer and Builder. The fact that from the first the prophet is sent by God "to pluck up and to break down . . . to build and to plant" is necessary to comprehend, if we are ever to grasp that the cross of Christ is both judgment and salvation for us, both death to the old ways and life anew.

Finally, the book of Jeremiah presents difficulties to the preacher by the very fact that it tells us so much about the prophet himself. In no other prophetic book do we have an extensive third-person biography of the prophet, and in no other prophetic work do we find autobiographical "confessions," unless one wants to take some of Second Isaiah's Servant Songs as reflective of that prophet's personal experience. We know almost too much about Jeremiah! The result is that the preacher is tempted to focus only on the figure of the prophet rather than on the Word of God that Jeremiah announces—again a tendency of the lectionary that uses the call narrative and confessions, along with a wisdom saying and the christological passages, to the exclusion of almost everything else. Contrary to the recent radical views of those like Robert Carroll, who sees the prophet largely as an ideal construct of the Deuteronomists' imagination, we can write something of a biography of the historical Jeremiah. The tendency of many preachers, therefore, is only to use the person of Jeremiah as an example of the struggles and suffering faced by those of faith and to ignore most of the message given in the prophet's preaching.

Certainly Jeremiah himself, in his struggles with God, is the legitimate subject of a sermon. Otherwise his "confessions" and his biography would not have been preserved in the canon. But that is not the only manner in which the preacher should utilize the Jeremianic materials, for the central subject of Jeremiah's book is much larger than the prophet. God is the main subject, and God's words and God's actions are finally all-important. The prophet himself has value for us only as he witnesses to his Lord and only as he carries out the tasks assigned to him by that Lord. To ignore

the words and working of God in and through the book of
Jeremiah is finally to misunderstand the prophet and to try
to interpret the world as Jeremiah himself never would have
interpreted it—as a secular place devoid of the divine influence and action. Thus, the first question the preacher should
ask of every passage in the book of Jeremiah is that question
that should always be asked of any biblical passage, "What is
God doing, according to this text?" And the answer to that
question, related to our life and faith, should then form the
principal subject of the sermon.

As stated above, Jeremiah's message leads almost inevi-
tably into the NT for one always has to ask, What became of
these ancient words? Was their promise of judgment or of salvation ever fulfilled in time? Or did they fall by the way into
the void and God's purposes spoken here remain uncom-
pleted? Similarly, one has to ask if the life of Israel reflected
in Jeremiah has analogy to the life of the new Israel, the
church, and can the church therefore learn from ancient Israel what it means to be God's covenant people? In short,
texts from Jeremiah should be used in sermons alongside
texts from the NT. Otherwise the witness to God in Jeremiah
and its import for his chosen people are never proclaimed in
their fullness, and the story of God's work in the world is left
suspended in the sixth century B.C.

As implied, Jeremiah texts can be paired with texts in the
NT in a scheme of promise and fulfillment, or by drawing
analogies between the life of Israel and of the church. (Israel,
it should be noted, is not to be made analogous to our nation
or any other. Israel is defined by the covenant relationship,
which finds its parallel in the new covenant given to the
church.) In addition, there is much in Jeremiah that can illumine texts in the NT, and this work tries to point out such
material, just as it also points to some places where the NT
illumines the OT. Or preachers can join the Testaments by
utilizing leading motifs—the figure of the "yoke" or of God as
a fountain of living waters, to give only two examples, play
prominent parts in Jeremiah and in the gospels. Occasion-
ally—perhaps rarely—legitimate contrasts can be drawn between OT and NT understandings, but the stereotyped view

of the OT as law and the NT as grace is, it is fervently hoped, a distortion now long discarded.

I first began studying and writing on Jeremiah for my M.Div. thesis as a student many years ago in seminary. For over thirty years, this prophet's message has informed and deepened my faith. He always has something new to offer; his treasure-store of the mysteries of God seems inexhaustible. And to preach from those mysteries seems to me to be the final challenge to and the reason for all Jeremiah studies. The preacher's art of proclaiming the Word remains the highest fruition of biblical scholarship. God grant that through our preaching, he may be made known to all people, from the least of them to the greatest.

The Call of the Prophet
(Jeremiah 1:4–10)

Despite the fact that this passage serves as the OT lesson for the fourth Sunday after Epiphany in some lectionaries, it has not been used as a sermon text very frequently in the church. The reason lies in the function of the text: it forms Jeremiah's autobiographical legitimization of his ministry, and the prophet probably set this passage at the beginning of that original collection of his prophecies that he dictated, and then re-dictated, to his scribe Baruch in 605 B.C. (see chap. 36). The time of his call is 627 B.C., and it is on the basis of this call, here recounted for us, that Jeremiah can say, "Thus says the Lord."

We modern-day Christians, however, are not called to be prophets, in the OT sense of the term, and it is important that the preacher be clear about this. For one thing, the Word of God is not given to us anew. Rather, we believe that the Word, incarnate in Jesus Christ, has now been fully spoken, and it is that Word which all Christian speaking and action now announce, explicate, and interpret for the church, in whatever age (see 1 Cor 2:2). We cannot add to the Word that God has said and done in Jesus Christ. We can only show what it means for our particular time and place.

Second, we do not share the prophetic experience of ecstasy, in which the prophet is allowed to stand in the heavenly council of the Lord, to be summoned to his ministry and to be given the Word that he is to speak (Jer 23:18, 22; see Isa 6:1–12; 40:1–8; 1 Kings 22:19–23). The Spirit works in the church, to be sure, and Christians still are given charismatic gifts, even speaking with tongues, but such gifts are not equivalent to OT prophetic ecstasy.

Third, the history of the OT prophets is not our history. We are far removed from them by time and place, by culture and worldview. The tasks to which they are called are related to their specific situation, and while analogies may be drawn between Israel's situation in relation to God and the church's, the two are not identical. We never exactly duplicate the prophets' experiences. Christians are not called to be prophets like Jeremiah, and so, in that sense, this passage is irrelevant for them.

What, then, can be the function of the passage for us? Obviously it has interest as part of the history of our salvation that culminates in God's act in Christ. But beyond that, the passage is revelatory of the God and Father of our Lord Jesus Christ. The passage is the beginning of the Jeremiah biography, but that must not be its focus. Its central character is God: Six times the word "Lord" appears in this text; its emphasis is on his Word and deed; its revelation is of a God immediately involved in his world, and that involvement is absolutely crucial for us.

Who is this God revealed through this call? First, he is a God of intimacy. There are no angelic mediators here, as in the calls of First and Second Isaiah (Isa 6:6–7; 40:1–8). God himself speaks to his prophet and himself touches his lips (vs. 9). He does not overwhelm Jeremiah with the vision of his transcendent glory (contrast Ezek 1; 3:15) or of his awesome moral purity (contrast Isa 6:5). He tells the prophet he has known him (vs. 5)—known him through and through, like a husband his wife or a father his son. Indeed, the Lord has formed Jeremiah in his mother's womb (vs. 5), like a potter shaping a piece of clay (see Job 10:8–11; Ps 139:13), fashioning the prophet's person and personality in muddy fingers and giving closest attention to the project. This God *intends* Jeremiah, and we readers have to ask in wonder if God has not also intently intended our creation.

It is to a youth (vs. 6) that this God of intimacy speaks—to a young man of marriageable age, about eighteen years old, who has never had any experience in public speaking in his life. God, it seems, chooses for his tasks not the mighty and prominent (see Deut 7:7), "not many wise, not many powerful, not many of noble birth," but those who are weak and foolish and low and despised in the world (1 Cor 1:26–27)— like that simple peasant girl, Mary of Nazareth. The God of glory lowers himself to the meekest and mildest and makes them his messengers and missioners to do his work in the world.

Over against the inadequacy of the instruments, God sets

his all-sufficiency. To Jeremiah's "I do not know," the Lord replies "I knew you" (vss. 6, 5); to Jeremiah's "I am only a
youth," God answers, "I am with you" (vss. 6, 8). "My grace is
sufficient for you, for my power is made perfect in weakness"
(2 Cor 12:9). Thus does God answer every hesitant excuse,
every fearful self-assessment, every self-serving attempt to
exempt ourselves from his mission.

The reason for that is clear. This God of Jeremiah's call is a
God with a purpose, and he creates human beings in his
world to serve that purpose. The purpose, says the Bible, has
been laid from the foundation of the world—to give abundant
life under his lordship to a creation that God simply loves
with all his heart and soul (see Gen 1; Jer 32:41; John 10:10).
Human beings have turned their back on God and on his good
gift of life and chosen evil and death instead (see Gen 2–11).
God therefore works unceasingly to turn humanity around—
to bring them back into fellowship with himself as their Lord,
that they may have abundant life from his hands.

God, the great Initiator, lays his plans very carefully to effect that turning or conversion: "Before I formed you . . . before you were born," he says to Jeremiah (vs. 5). God's plan to
use Jeremiah in his service precedes even the prophet's conception in the womb. And then the plan is worked out in three
stages: "I knew," "I consecrated," "I appointed" (vs. 5). Jeremiah is set apart in the purpose of God—for such is the meaning of "consecrated"—to fulfill one task for God in the world:
to be a prophet to the nations in the years 626 B.C. to about
584 B.C. That is the meaning of Jeremiah's existence, the reason God has made him and brought him into being, and Jeremiah's life henceforth makes sense only as he serves that
purpose.

Paul possessed the same sense of call (Rom 1:1) and found
no reason for living unless he heeded the summons (see 1 Cor
9:16). But that apostle was also convinced that all Christians
possess a similar call to specific tasks within the church and
the world that will further God's purposed plan (Rom 8:28–
30; 9:24; 1 Cor 1:26; 7:17; Gal 1:6; 5:8, etc.). It is therefore
questionable whether any Christian can know a sense of
meaning for his or her life, or ever escape a restless heart,
apart from serving that purpose for which God has created

him or her in the beginning. God plans us for tasks in church and society, and we know no peace unless we serve that intention.

So there is a compulsion imposed upon Jeremiah here, a compulsion he later tries desperately but futilely to escape (see Jer 20:9), and in that fact is recognition not only of an intimate God but also of a sovereign Lord. Jeremiah acknowledges as much: "Ah, Adonai Yahweh," he exclaims in vs. 6, that is, "Ah, Master," or "Ah, Owner." We are God's possession and the sheep of his pasture (Ps 100:3) and never can human beings be fully understood apart from that relationship (see Gen 1:26–28). For those who confess the relationship, the fact is comfort and joy (see Jer 15:16); for those who rebel against it or try to deny it, it is a burden (15:17) and a goad (see Acts 26:14).

God as sovereign Lord over his creature speaks in commandments: "To all to whom I send you you shall go, and whatever I command you you shall speak." "Go!" "Make disciples!" "Baptize!" "Teach!" (Matt 28:19–20, author's paraphrase)—the command has always been pronounced, by a God who is restlessly, constantly moving human life forward toward his good outcome for it. God is not the God of the status quo—never a benign and mystical Presence simply to be enjoyed by his creatures—but a God on the move, ceaselessly at work, calling and sending and commanding. Where true God is met, a task is given and its fulfillment expected.

But always this sovereign, commanding God equips his servants for their jobs. Jeremiah not only hears that but also sees it and feels it. The divine hand is stretched forth, the prophet's lips are touched by the hand, and the Word is thereby given the prophet to speak. (There is no indication here, as there is in Isa 6:7, that the prophet's lips must be cleansed.) Jeremiah's future preaching is not the result of his own reflection—not the product of his analysis of Judah's social and international situation—not the conviction of his own mind and conscience. Human mind and conscience and insight, bent as they always are by self-interest and sin, would never have conceived Jeremiah's message. The wisdom of God appears always foolishness to the world (1 Cor 1:20–25; see Jer 20:10; 17:15), and so it must come from outside the world—

from God himself. God must equip a prophet with words (see
Isa 50:4), as he must equip every Christian with a love and a
faith and a hope that we do not possess in ourselves (1 Cor
12:31–13:13). The ability to do the commanded task comes as
gift from God (Eph 4:11–14). Thus, the gift is always adequate
to the task, but it remains a gift. We recipients of God's gifts
can never claim, in our pride, that our abilities to do God's
work in the world stem from our own capabilities. We never
possess those capabilities in ourselves, apart from our relation to God in Christ. He is the vine; we are the branches;
apart from him we can do nothing (John 15:5).

This God of Jeremiah sends his prophet to do a double task
in his world: "to pluck up and to break down," but also "to
build and to plant" (vs. 10; the middle line, "to destroy and
to overthrow," is probably an addition to the text, since it de-
stroys the chiasmus). Those two functions—of judgment and
salvation—given to Jeremiah to preach, always constitute
the work of God in human life, according to the entire Bible,
and neither is to be separated from the other. The reasons are
very clear.

God always has to destroy the old life—the ways of the
world, the status quo—because human life is shot through
with sin, and God will not countenance sin. He will not accept for his creatures less than they were created to be,
namely, his beloved people living in a community of justice
and righteousness, of peace and joy, under his lordly direction. He will not give his beloved ones over to meaningless-
ness and captivity to wrong and perpetual strife and final
death. He will not surrender his sovereignty over his creation
or let his purpose of good come to naught. As the prophet
Ezekiel has spoken it, God "will be king over" us (20:33), and
to be that, he will tirelessly pluck up and break down the
rebellious and sinful ways we have devised, until he has fash-
ioned us into a people pleasing to him, "without spot or
wrinkle or any such thing . . . holy and without blemish" (Eph
5:27). That is always the work of the God of love, who desires
that we have life and have it more abundantly.

Before there can be a new life, the old life must be destroyed; before there can be a resurrection, there must be a
crucifixion. The grain of wheat must fall in the ground and

die before it can bring forth fruit. The new wine cannot be put into old wineskins, nor the new patch sewn on the old garment. Any preaching that proclaims the salvation of God apart from his judgment has ignored an essential half of the biblical message, and preachers only of comfort and healing and success are condemned by the Scriptures (Jer 6:14; 8:11). So the youthful Jeremiah is sent to pluck up and break down Judah's sinful ways.

Jeremiah will carry out that task by means of his preaching. The reader must understand the nature of the Word of God in the prophetic literature, and indeed in all of the Bible, in order to comprehend Jeremiah's task. The Word, in the Bible's understanding, is active, effective force, which brings about events and changes situations (see Gen 1:3; Isa 55:10–11; Ezek 12:28). The Word of God not only calls to repentance and gives new understanding, but it also works in human life until it brings about that of which it speaks. Thus, when Jeremiah announces judgment on Judah, the Word of God, spoken by the prophet, sets events in motion, that will finally issue in the destruction of Judah in 587 B.C.

It is no wonder, therefore, that Jeremiah is also told, "Be not afraid of them" (vs. 8), for Jeremiah's message of judgment really consists in the announcement that God has declared war against Judah. We shall see that declaration of war spelled out in the stunning messages of judgment that follow. For the moment, suffice it to say that we have here, in Jeremiah's call, traditional language of the Israelite Holy War, dating back to the time when Israel was a tribal federation (1220–1020 B.C.) and then preserved in the prophetic traditions of the Northern Kingdom and especially in Deuteronomy. And part of that tradition is the divine imperative, "Be not afraid of them," as is the reason for the imperative: God himself fights for the prophet and will deliver him from his foes (vs. 8; see Deut 3:22; 7:18; 20:1, 3; 31:6, 8). But foes there will be! No one who calls the status quo into question can escape criticism and opposition, especially if he or she claims to represent the position of God, and especially if that judgment gets down to the particulars of privilege and vested interest and pride and popular ideology. All persons create shells to protect themselves against criticism, and they do not like those shells to be broken, especially by their religious leaders.

The Christian pulpit certainly is called to the prophetic function of criticism and judgment. However, John C. Bennett, that most balanced of theologians of the last generation, issued a warning to all modern-day "prophetic" preachers in a sermon he gave on this text. His words bear quotation:

> ... prophets very easily become self-righteous and unlovely. I remember a saying that went the rounds some years ago to the effect that one can define a saint as the wife of a prophet. Prophets who emphasize the negative side of their message often become single-track and very poor guides. They are inclined to identify their own convictions, even on difficult political issues, with the judgment of God. There are in Christian faith correctives for this tendency, but only too often they do not take effect. The prophets should realize that they also are under judgment, that they also have their own special temptations, their own way of becoming, like the cedars of Lebanon, high and lifted up.... Most often confession with the people rather than denunciation of the people should be the way in which the prophet speaks ("The Prophetic Side of Christianity, (1 Kings 22:8; Jer. 1:9–10))," *Best Sermons*, (ed. by G. Paul Butler; New York: McGraw-Hill, 1955), p. 280.

Let it be emphasized that Bennett is speaking to Christian preachers, and Jeremiah's role was somewhat different from theirs. Jeremiah had to proclaim God's denunciations and could not simply identify with his people in their sin. He was forced to stand "against the whole land" (1:18), and to be sure, that sometimes led even him into sinful pride (15:15–21). But he really had no wish to call down God's destruction on his wayward people (17:16), and he was grieved to the heart over Judah's ruin (8:18–9:1). Nevertheless, he could not escape his obligation to announce the Lord's war against his people.

The other half of Jeremiah's task makes both the prophet's mission and the judging function of the church meaningful, however. Jeremiah was called also "to build and to plant" (vs. 10), and that command should never be separated from the first, "to pluck up and to break down." Once again, in Bennett's words,

The Christian Church is called to mediate both the judgment and the forgiveness of God to the same people, at the same time—to be at once prophet, pastor, and priest (ibid, pp. 280–81).

Indeed, throughout Jeremiah and the rest of the Scripture, God's judgment is a work of his love, because it is an action designed to make God's people anew. Judgment is always finally for the purpose of salvation. God never judges simply to punish or to take vengeance on his own. God plucks up in order to plant; he breaks down in order to rebuild. He does away with the old life in order to create a new one. His goal of restoring abundant life to his creation always shapes and guides his actions. As a consequence, Paul can write that God works in everything for good for those called according to his purpose (Rom 8:28). Jeremiah, despite his anguish over the ruin of his people, can set his face steadfastly toward the future. And the Christian preacher who, together with his people, confesses "there is no health in us," can joyfully look for that healing balm of Gilead that God in his mercy will surely give. The judgment of God is never a separate Word. It is never the last Word. Rather, it is a necessary Word, given that we may be saved.

Two Visions
(Jeremiah 1:11–19)

Although these two visions have been attached to the original call of Jeremiah, they really do not belong with 1:4–10 (note "a second time" in 1:13). The vision of vss. 13–19, probably to be dated in 609–605 B.C., forms the prologue to Jeremiah's oracles on the Foe from the North (which see), and should be interpreted in that context. The brief vision of vss. 11–12 has been attached inseparably to vs. 13, however, by its identical structure. Probably vss. 15b–16 are Deuteronomic elaborations of the vision of vss. 13–15a, but they are now bound inseparably with it by the contrast between the "evil" that God calls out of the north (vs. 14) and the "evil" (RSV: "wickedness") of the people (vs. 16). Verses 17–19 are also probably a Deuteronomic elaboration of 1:7–8, but they are now joined inextricably with vs. 16 by their emphatic "But you" (vs. 17), and this in turn contrasts with "But I" (in Hebrew) at the beginning of vs. 18. The rhetorical structure of the passage supports its present unity.

These visions have been put here because they both enlarge on the nature of Jeremiah's original call. We should be clear about their interpretation, however.

First, vss. 11–12 are not to be understood as some sort of revelation of God through nature. "God is for ever teaching us from the Book of Nature as the bright pages pass," enthused one preacher (James Rutherford, *The Seer's House and Other Sermons* [Edinburgh: T. and T. Clark, 1914] p. 295). To this, we must answer, "No!" The almond branch (*shaqed*), with its early white January blossoms has no meaning for the prophet apart from God's interpreting word. According to the Scriptures, the Creator can never be found or fully known through his creation, because he is qualitatively Other from it, that is, he is Holy God (see Isa 40:18; Hos 11:9; 1 Kings 8:27). So God himself must explain, in a word-play, that he is watching (*shoqed*) over his Word to perform it.

We do not know when God told Jeremiah this. Perhaps it was in that desperate period of the prophet's life when both he and his compatriots doubted that the Word would ever be fulfilled (17:14–18). But now that assurance has been set for us at the beginning of the story of Jeremiah's struggles, and we are to remember it as we read further. God keeps his Word. He is deadly serious about what his prophets say. All that Jeremiah speaks will come to pass. And all that God speaks to us through his prophets, and all that he has finally spoken by a Son (Heb 1:1–2), will also come to pass. He might have added, "Let him who has ears to hear, hear!"

There follows a frightful message in vss. 13–16: God is declaring war against his own people. Though the text is difficult, in ecstatic vision Jeremiah is given to see a boiling pot in the north, with its fearsome brew bubbling southward toward Judah, symbolic of the fact that God is calling all the tribes of the kingdoms of the north to war against his covenant people and finally to lay siege to Jerusalem (vs. 15). The kingdoms of the north are not named, and indeed they have no name. They are symbols of God's warfare against his own people, later enfleshed in the troops of Babylonia. But God is the attacker—that is the important point. While 1:8 used the language of the Holy War, the full scenario is here spelled out. God comes, first of all, not to save his people but to destroy them. He begins his promised work of plucking up and breaking down (1:10).

The reason for that divine warfare is clear: the people have broken the first commandment by committing idolatry. In place of the worship of their Creator they have put the worship of their own creations (vs. 16; see Rom 1:25). But God must be loved and worshiped with all our hearts and minds and strength (Deut 6:5), or we have substituted lesser gods for him in our lives. Because God loves us with all his heart and wishes for us the highest good, he cannot and he will not permit any substitution for his lordship to take place.

"The Lord is with me as a dread warrior," Jeremiah said (20:11). Biblical faith knows such a God, who wars against every individual and corporate challenge to his rule, until he subdues and defeats it. If that be not true, human evil will have the last word in our world. But it is true; and so God's warfare—even against his church—is good news for the faithful. Evil cannot win, for God fights it, here in Jeremiah's time and through all the sacred history, until finally he wins the decisive victory over it at the site of an empty tomb.

Because God goes to war against wickedness, every person must choose, however—whether in every decision and deed to be with God or against him (Luke 11:14–23, esp. vs. 23). There is no neutral ground in the fray, no middle alternative. The choice is either life or death (Deut 30:15), the broad way or the narrow (Matt 7:13–14). And so it is too with Jeremiah. Because the whole populace of Judah has lost its allegiance to its Lord (see Jer 5:1–5), God is against them all—rulers, religious leaders, ordinary citizens (1:18)—and Jeremiah must choose a side. If he is undone by the resulting loneliness, opposition, and persecution, and begins to waffle on his commitment to God, the dread Warrior will destroy him in the eyes of his compatriots (vs. 17). Jeremiah's awful choice is between a God he loves and a society he loves—a choice not unknown to the Christian. How enjoyable the ways of so much of our common life and yet how also in need of God's transformation!

Fortunately Jeremiah does not make his choice between God or society out of his own strength alone. "I appoint you" (vs. 18; RSV: "make you") this day," God tells his prophet. And we too do not make the choice, but God chooses us (John 15:16), to "gird up," "arise," "speak," "do not be dismayed" (vs. 17). God chooses us to bear fruit for his gospel in the world, and always he gives that ultimate equipment of his Word (vs. 17) and the never-failing promise: "I am with you, says the Lord, to deliver you" (vs. 19; see Matt 28:20). So we act and speak and think and make decisions not on our own and never only according to our tempted desires or only by our limited vision out of our own shaky confidence. But we play the part of the Christian in the world by the choice and equipment and strengthening of the Word, Jesus Christ. "It is no longer I who live, but Christ who lives in me" (Gal 2:20). Upon that fellowship with God rests all biblical faith and action.

The Early Preaching
(Jeremiah 2:1–37)

This chapter is made up of five separate oracles: 2:2b–3 +
20–22; 2:4–13; 2:14–19; 2:23–28, and 2:29–37. All of them
originally belonged to the earliest period of Jeremiah's
preaching (626–621 B.C.), although the references to Egypt in
vss. 16 and 36 have updated two of the poems to the time
when Egyptian dominance over Judah ended and Jeremiah
re-dictated his prophecies (in 605 B.C.; see 36:27–32). All of
the oracles are framed in terms of a court case, with God pre-
senting his indictments against Judah for her breaches of the
covenant relationship. And all of these poems share Deuteronomy's concern for the intimate nature of the covenant relation and its breach by apostasy. These oracles provide the
preacher with the opportunity to examine in depth the relation between God and his people.

Behind all these poems lies Judah's sin of Baal worship,
and the preacher must therefore understand something of Canaanite religion. Common to all of the non-Judaic religions of
the ancient Near East was the belief that the life of the gods
was bound up with and revealed through the natural realm.
Conflicts in nature mirrored conflicts among the gods; har-
mony there portrayed divine relationships. Consequently, any
aspect of creation could become a medium of divine revelation—trees, stones, wooden poles (in our day, the beauty of
lakes and mountains). Human life took its pattern from the
cycle of birth, life, and death in nature, endlessly repeated,
and the goal of worship therefore was so to coerce and participate in that cycle, through the use of sympathetic magic in
the cult, that life, prosperity, and fertility would prevail over
death, want, and barrenness. Sacred prostitution in the cult
was frequent practice, because it was believed that the exercise of fertility between humans would coerce the production
of that fertility in nature. Similarly, it was believed that the
divine could be coerced to give prosperity and protection
from enemies by the sacrifice of the first-born child, and ar-
chaeology has found evidence of such sacrifices in the corner-

stones of Canaanite houses and city walls. But basic to it all was the belief that the gods were contained in and revealed through various aspects of the created world.

Biblical faith, especially as found in the prophetic writings and Deuteronomy, represented a sharp attack against such baalistic beliefs. The God of Israel is not contained in or revealed through any part of the natural world (see the second commandment of the Decalogue; Deuteronomy's emphasis on the oneness of God [6:4] over against the diffuse numina of the Canaanites; and its emphasis on the Word as the sole means of revelation [4:12]). God is the Lord over creation, who can never be coerced; and he can be known by human beings only as he enters into relationship with his people and reveals himself through his own words and actions (see Deut 4:32–35). Judah's practice of Baal worship, therefore, was a fundamental denial of the nature and will of the true God, just as modern attempts to equate him with some sort of "birthing goddess," from whose being all things have come forth, is a similar fundamental denial. The qualitative otherness of the Creator from his creation is never softened in the Bible.

Given those facts, we are now in a position to understand God's indictments against Judah in Jer 2. All of these poems share common motifs, but there are emphases in each that the pulpit can use.

The Nature of the Covenant Relationship (2:2b–3 + 20–22)

No oracle better sets forth the nature of the covenant relationship: it has the character of a marriage, with God in love with his youthful bride, and Judah the bride in love with him. If we want to know what attitude and action God expects from us, then those of a faithful wife toward her husband are held up to us by this passage. Intimate knowledge, daily companionship, mutual labor, and honor and faithfulness—those are the qualities of marital love, according to the OT (see Gen 2:18–25; Mal 2:14–16), and so too the expected nature of the relation with God. God here wistfully remembers his honeymoon time with his bride—as in Hosea, the time in the wilderness, before Judah went after other lovers, the Baals. The metaphor explodes all our stereotypes about the God of the OT as some sort of legalistic and wrathful despot. God, the lover of his people, asks from them faithful love in return (see Deut 6:5 et passim).

In the second strophe of the poem (vs. 3), the figure changes, to emphasize God's protection of his people. Israel is the first fruits of God's grape harvest (see vs. 21). By covenant law, all first fruits of produce belonged to God (Exod 23:19) and were set aside in the cult as provision for the priests. For non-priests to eat such fruits was a most heinous sin (see Lev 22:9). Thus, in the metaphor of this strophe, any who attacked Israel incurred guilt before God (see the Amalekites; Exod 17:8–14). Jeremiah is emphasizing God's sheltering care of his people, but he is also pointing out that Israel is a nation set apart (which is the meaning of "holy") for sole use by God (see Exod 19:4–6; Num 23:9). In short, Israel is loved by God, not for privilege only, but also for responsibility. God has a purpose, which he wants to work out through his chosen people (see Gen 12:3 for the purpose), and only as Israel follows God (vs. 2) can she fulfill the purpose for which in fact she was created.

With love comes responsibility. Reinhold Niebuhr once made the profound statement that love is the willingness to take responsibility (see the refusal of Adam and Eve to do so; Gen 3:11–13). Jeremiah symbolizes this in the figure of the "yoke" in vs. 20 (2:20–22 continue the two figures of speech found in 2:2b–3 and are bound to it by the connecting "for," vs. 20). In the life of faith, there is a yoke to be worn, a discipline to follow. "Take my yoke upon you," Jesus said (Matt 11:29). Love for God is never unbridled freedom, either individual or corporate. As in Gen 2:17, paradise is obedience. Indeed, in the thought of the Bible there is no "individual freedom." We are slaves either of sin, says Paul, or of Jesus Christ. We are called to "follow" God, like a faithful wife her husband, or—changing the figure—we are asked to heed the Master Farmer's guiding reins, lest we wander off into some corn patch of sin and become too bloated and sick to serve God's planting.

So the preacher has a marvelous opportunity here to explore the covenant relationship with God, into which the church has entered through Jesus Christ (1 Cor 11:23). It is a relationship of the most intimate, protecting, tender, and faithful love. But it is also a relationship of obedience and discipline in daily life.

The difficulty is, of course, that we all think we are obedient. Few persons set out deliberately to do wrong. Most church members sincerely want to lead a faithful Christian life, and indeed, most of us think we are doing so. As a companion piece to 2:2b–3, 20–22, the preacher may therefore want to look at the following:

The Unyoked Life (2:23–28)

Here the prophet explores the fact, as he will so often (see, for example, 8:6–7), that our sin lames our self-assessment. "How can you say, O covenant people," he asks incredulously, "that you have not gone after the Baals and have not broken your yoke?" (vs. 23, author's paraphrase). Few of us ever believe that we are really, truly sinners. For one thing, our sin has always looked like the right thing to do at the time (see Gen 3:6); for another, we usually have good excuses for our actions (see Gen 3:11–13). "My parents didn't raise me right;" "I've got this psychological hangup;" "I got mixed up in the wrong crowd (or environment)." And so Jeremiah lays out God's court case against his people.

The figures of speech are not pretty. He compares us disobedient, unyoked creatures to a wild camel, criss-crossing the desert aimlessly (vs. 23), or to a wild ass, lusting in her heat after a mate (vs. 24). They do not seem like figures that one can properly use in a sermon. And yet, apart from God's yoke we do become like beasts—driven by the fads and follies of the world or our own desires, acting in beastly fashion in our selfishness toward family and neighbors, wearing ourselves out in frantic pursuit of some mythical "good life," when all along, abundant life is to be had only from our guiding Lord.

The prophet draws on the traditions of Deuteronomy here to contrast the yoked life with the unyoked (vs. 25). Deuteronomy and Jeremiah both emphasize the terrors of the wilderness—a place of drought and pits and deep darkness, where no man dwells (Jer 2:6). And, says Deuteronomy, God disciplined and cared for his people in that "terrible wilderness" (Deut 1:19), like a Father disciplining and caring for his beloved son (Deut 1:31; 8:5). He kept their backs clothed and their feet shod (Deut 29:5), and provided for all their needs, giving them food from heaven and water from a rock (8:3, 15), showing them where to pitch their tents (1:31–33). For forty years, he accompanied them, and because he was there, they lacked no necessity (Deut 2:7), just as God has provided for the necessities of the church down through the ages. And now, asks Jeremiah, will you give up all that? "Keep your feet from going unshod," he pleads, "and your throat from thirst" (2:25). "Take my yoke upon you, and learn from me, for I am gentle and lowly in heart, and you will find rest for your souls." But Judah's reply, as often ours, is that of freedom from the easy yoke: "It is hopeless, for I have loved other things and other gods and other ways more than you, and it is to them that I will dedicate my life and love" (vs. 25, author's paraphrase).

What follows in vss. 26–28, therefore, is God's verdict on his unrepentant people. He gives them over to the unyoked life they have chosen for themselves. (The classic NT witness to God's "giving us over" to our sins is found in Rom 1:24–32.) If wilderness is what we want, then God's judgment is that wilderness is what we shall have. And when the sun beats down, and our throats are parched, and we have lost our way, we can vainly call on our worthless idols to give us shelter and drink and direction (vs. 28). Perhaps the church needs more often to hear this verdict on its unyoked "freedom."

Two of the metaphors that Jeremiah uses here—water and wilderness—bring us, however, to the centerpiece of chapter 2.

Apostasy and Uselessness (2:4–13)

In this famous oracle too, God presents his case in court against Israel (vs. 9; "contend" means "go to law"). God is the plaintiff as well as the prosecutor, and the heavens are the jury (vs. 12). The indictment is directed against all Israel, past, present, and future (vs. 4). Thus, this is a case directed not only at the Israel of the old covenant, but by analogy at the new Israel in Christ, the church.

Israel is charged with two offenses: she has "forsaken" her Lord (vss. 13, 4), and she has gone after "worthlessness" (vs. 4) or "that which does not profit" (vss. 8, 11, 13). So sin is a twofold aberration: a desertion of the God with whom we share loving intimacy in the covenant relation; and a seeking out of other things and gods to take his place. We apparently cannot live in a devotional vacuum very long. If we desert God, we always give our devotion to something else (see Luke 11:24–26).

But this oracle hammers home the utter futility of love for other than God. There are four stanzas in the poem—vss. 4–6, 7–8, 9–11, and 12–13, and each of them emphasizes that futility. The thought is summarized at the beginning of stanza one (vs. 4): Israel went after (literally) "emptiness," that is, other gods, and so herself became "empty"—we become what we worship. Each of the following stanzas then ends with the same thought. Israel went after (literally) "that which is useless" (vs. 8e); she changed her glory "for that which is useless" (vs. 11); she dug for herself "broken cisterns that can hold no water" (vs. 13e), in short, that are useless. Empty, useless—such are the idols we worship. They do nothing, see nothing, hear nothing, demand nothing, give nothing.

Over against such vain recipients of our devotion, Jeremiah places the actions and character of the God of the covenant. He recalls the central events in Israel's past life: the exodus redemption (vs. 6), God's guidance of her through the wilderness (vs. 6), and God's gift to her of the promised land (vs. 7). This is no dead and useless deity, but the Lord who can make a promise and then keep it—the Lord who takes a people for himself in love and then who has the power to put that love into effect. This God speaks, acts, demands (vs. 8). Indeed, this God gives life: he is like a fountain of living waters, an ever-flowing stream in the desert (vs. 13), who quenches the thirst of our souls and relieves us in the heat of the day and sustains us alive through every peril, in the face of death (see John 4:10–14). And that is the "glory" of the covenant people (vs. 11), in OT and NT, that they have such a God who keeps his promises to them and works out his purpose for them and sustains them with his water of life all along the way.

To forsake such a God, therefore, and to substitute for his bubbling fountain of life our own useless, self-made deities—leaky cisterns in the desert!—is obviously the height of stupidity. Why would we do such a thing? Why choose death instead of life? God, through his prophet, simply cannot understand such folly. Did you find something wrong in me? he asks Israel (vs. 4). Has any other nation ever deserted its god (vs. 11)? The questions concern the mysterious power of sin and finally are unanswerable. There is no rhyme or reason to our choice of death in place of life. Given a garden, we choose desert (Gen 3), and thirst and heat and fainting, as frantically we look for water from the useless deities of our own making.

We might term this poem an OT presentation of the doctrine of original sin, and through most of his career Jeremiah will struggle with the problem of such sin. What can overcome it? He will finally arrive at an answer (31:31–34). But for now, his emphasis is clear: to worship other than the Lord yields emptiness, worthlessness, desert, death.

False Reliance on Other Nations (2:14–19)

Verse 16 of this poem probably refers to the death of King Josiah of Judah at the battle of Megiddo in 609 B.C., when Egypt marched north to try to aid the Assyrian Empire in its battle against Babylonia. The poem in its present form therefore dates from the time when Judah was a vassal to Egypt, 609–605 B.C.

It has been put in its present position because it picks up key words from and enlarges on the thought of 2:4–13. Specifically, it enlarges the definition of what it means to "forsake" God (vss. 17, 19). In the preceding oracle, Judah forsook the Lord to go after other gods (vs. 13). Here she forsakes him by relying on foreign nations and their military for her security. For God's way, Judah has substituted the "way" to Egypt and, earlier, Assyria (vss. 17, 18). For her redemption from Egypt (vs. 6), she has substituted slavery once again (vs. 14). For God's life-giving water (vs. 13), she has substituted foreign waters (vs. 18). But those waters will prove evil and bitter as her sin returns upon her own head (vs. 19). There are, however, other passages in the OT much better suited to point out that international relations can constitute a form of apostasy (see Isa 30:1–5; 31:1–3).

Failure to Repent and Obey (2:29–37)

This oracle too picks up the motifs that we found earlier in chapter 2: the inexplicable nature of sin (vss. 31–32), Judah's obliviousness to it (vs. 35), her apostasy in forsaking the Lord (vs. 31) for foreign gods (vs. 33) and alliances (vs. 36), all in the setting of God's court case against his people (vs. 35). Three new notes briefly appear: reference to Judah's failure to accept God's correction of them by means of the prophets' words, and reference to the murder of prophets in the time of Manasseh (vs. 30); an allusion to injustice in the law courts toward the innocent poor (vs. 34); and just a hint of the exile (vs. 37). All are treated more fully elsewhere in Jeremiah.

Repentance True and False
(Jeremiah 3:1—4:4)

A number of oracles from various times and origins have been placed together here to deal with the subject of repentance. 3:1–5; 3:19–20, and 4:1–4 are all directed toward Judah and Jerusalem and probably date from 626–621 B.C. 3:6–11 is a Deuteronomic comment on 3:1–5, showing that the Southern Kingdom of Judah is guiltier of apostasy than was the Northern Kingdom of Israel, because Judah did not learn from Israel's exile to Assyria in 722/1 B.C. 3:12–13 proclaim God's willingness to forgive exiled northern Israel if she confesses her sin, and 3:21–23 picture such confession, to which is attached a Deuteronomic expansion in 3:24–25. 3:14–17, 18 are promises directed to exiled Judah after 587 B.C.

False and True Commitment (3:1–5, 19–20)

God is incensed by phony commitment and reliance on cheap grace: such is the thrust of 3:1–5. Judah is a religious people here, addressing God as her Father (3:4a), claiming an ongoing relationship with him from her earliest days (3:4; the Hebrew has two sentences: "Have you not just now called me, 'My Father'? A companion of my youth art thou"). Moreover, Judah is sure that God will forgive her, no matter what she does (3:5), much in the manner of modern-day worshipers who believe that God will always forgive. But the Lord, through his prophet, cites two facts to contradict such careless views.

First, 3:1 refers to the law of Deut 24:1–4, which states that a divorced woman who marries another cannot return to her first husband, if she is divorced by the second or even if he dies. She has been "defiled" by the second husband, and her return to her first husband would "pollute" the whole land, by defying the commandment of God. 3:1d–2 then point out that Judah has not only a second "husband," but dozens of them in the form of the Baal gods. She has deserted her divine husband and even lain in wait, like some Arab robber in the wilderness, to lie with her lovers. Yet, when she gets into trouble, she expects to return to her divine husband, God.

Second, because Judah has broken her covenant commitment to the Lord, He has brought upon her his covenant curse in the form of drought (vs. 3ab; see Deut 28:22–24; Jer 12:4; 14:1–10). But rather than taking that warning judgment seriously, Judah has refused even to be ashamed (vs. 3cd). God loves her, she thinks, no matter what, and so anything goes. She can always count on "good ole God" to accept her, welcome her, and succor her in time of trouble.

Judah's is a faith of words divorced from deeds, a superficial commitment uninvolved with her heart. Hers is a marriage of convenience, entered into for whatever she can get out of it; and while she expects her divine husband to fulfill all his commitments to the marital relation, she has no intention of fulfilling hers. How strongly we would condemn anyone who entered a human marriage with such an attitude, but the witness of Jer 3:1–5 is that such is our attitude toward God.

In strongest contrast, 3:19–20 pictures the commitment of God. The figure changes to that of the father-son relationship, in 3:19, but then returns to that of the marital covenant in vs. 20. Verse 19 is awe-inspiring—God dreaming of a future for Judah—of how he would make Judah one of his children, fit to be a member of his family; of how he would pass on to that beloved adopted son a beautiful piece of land in Palestine as an inheritance; of how that child would love him and run after him and call out to him, "Father!" Does not every father turn over in his mind such dreams for his children? And is it not incredible, then, for the Father to find that we have nothing of the love for him that he has for us—that we feel no obligation or lasting affection toward him? Jeremiah pictures the depth of our sin in the light of the love of God.

Circumcision of the Heart (3:12–13, 21–24; 4:1–4)

Despite all—despite our superficial loyalty, our idolatry, our breach of covenant commitment (see above)—God the Father, God the divine Husband cherishes us and yearns for our return to him. Jeremiah spells out that mercy in two oracles to the exiled Northern Kingdom of Israel. The first,

3:12–13, is a call to a faithless wife. The second, 3:21–24, pleads with faithless sons. In both, the incredible offer of forgiveness is extended. The covenant still stands, proclaims 3:12, which reads in the Hebrew of its third line, "for *hesed* I am," that is, "faithful to my covenant with you." God still holds open the door for return (3:12, 22), even though northern Israel has been so faithless that God has had to send them into Assyrian exile. His is a love that will not let them go. Yet, one thing is necessary for their return to him: acknowledgment of their sin (3:13). Israel must realize that she has been unfaithful, that she has gone after other gods, that her old way of life is unacceptable—in short, she must repent and turn around and live a new life acceptable to her divine Husband. There is no easy forgiveness here, no acceptance of the status quo. Repentance involves an alteration of lifestyle, else it is false repentance, unacceptable to God (see 3:4–5).

Thus, in 3:21–24, Jeremiah pictures true repentance: weeping supplication to the Father (vs. 21), full acknowledgment of past idolatry and disobedience (vss. 23–25), sincere confession that from God alone come salvation and life (vs. 23).

This sincere repentance on the part of the Northern Kingdom, then, is placed in its present position as a model for southern Judah, and in 4:1–4, Judah too is invited to return—in her situation, before her punishment and exile become necessary (vs. 4). Once again, her repentance must involve a changed life. She must put away her idolatry, firmly and unwaveringly (vs. 1), and claim the Lord as the only God, truthfully, by living according to his order (RSV: "justice") for society and by fulfilling his covenant demand for trust in him alone (RSV: "righteousness") (vs. 2).

The Lord and Judah both have a lot at stake in this call for repentance. Not only will Judah avoid God's judgment on her sin (vs. 4), but she will also once again become the instrument through whom God can bring his blessing on all the "families of the earth" (vs. 2cd; see Gen 12:3). God created his covenant people in the first place, in order that he might save the world through them. If Judah will be faithful to her covenant commitment, God can fulfill that purpose of love. And really, Judah's existence has no meaning apart from that task of being God's instrument of salvation. In short, God is offering her here not only life, but also purpose for living. What more could she desire?

The response she must make to God's merciful offer is detailed in 3:3-4, and both verses point to the involvement of Judah's heart. Judah inwardly is like an unplowed field, says Jeremiah. Her heart is hard, sun-baked, arid, crusted over, yielding only thorn-bushes. Plow it up with repentance, proclaims the prophet, that God may sow and reap through you! Or, in the other figure, Judah's heart is uncircumcised, stubbornly refusing any mark that she belongs to God (see Deut 10:16; Gen 17:11). By repentance, acknowledge that you are God's and God's alone, pleads the prophet.

This call for the transformation of Judah's heart forms the central proclamation of Jeremiah and, indeed, is the principal covenant demand laid on Israel by most of the prophets. God wants our hearts. He wants our love, our devotion to him from our most inward parts—our cleaving to him with the love of a faithful wife for her husband, our dependence on him and trust in him like that of a child for his father; for out of that love and trust will flow obedience and gratitude and service. Then God will use us as his instruments to bring all peoples back to himself, and his kingdom will have come on earth, even as it is in heaven.

The Word to the Heart
(Jeremiah 4:5–9:9)

This section in Jeremiah contains much of the preaching that the prophet did between 622 and 605 B.C. We find here the collection of Jeremiah's oracles on the Foe from the North: 4:5–8; 4:13–18; 4:29–31; 5:15–17; 6:1–8; 6:22–26, and 8:14–17. (A fragment is found also in 10:22.) All of these date probably from 609–605 B.C., during the period of Egyptian domination of Judah. Jeremiah's call to deliver these oracles is given in 1:13–15 (see above), while his reaction to their words is found in 4:19–22; 8:18–9:1 and, most extremely, in 4:23–26.

At the same time, many oracles are also found in this section that date from 622/1 B.C., when King Josiah inaugurated the Deuteronomic reform (see 2 Kings 22–23; 2 Chron 34–35), until the death of Josiah and the beginning of the reign of Jehoiakim in 609 B.C. These include 5:1–9; 5:20–29; 6:9–12; 6:13–15; 6:16–21; 6:27–30; 8:4–7; 8:8–13, while in 7:16–20; 7:21–8:3, and 9:2–9, we find God's reactions to Judah's actions during this period.

Interrupting the section is Jeremiah's famous Temple Sermon, in 7:1–15, that was delivered at the beginning of Jehoiakim's reign in 609 or 608 B.C. That sermon will be dealt with below, as a separate unit.

Found, too, in this section are a number of fragments: 4:9–10, 11–12, 28; 5:12–14, 30–31, some of which have to do with false prophecy. And there are a few later insertions, which promise that the Lord will not make a full end of Judah: 4:27; 5:18.

Usually scholars have considered 4:5–6:30 + 8:14–17 to be an early collection within the book, but probably 4:5–9:9 are the proper boundaries, with 7:1–15, plus other materials in 7:16–8:3, inserted in 605 B.C. into the collection (compare 9:9 with 5:9, 29).

The Foe from the North (4:5–8, 13–18, 29–31; 5:15–17; 6:1–8, 22–26; 8:14–17 [10:22])

What should a preacher do with Jeremiah's oracles on the Foe from the North? Usually the pulpit has ignored them as unworthy portions of the Christian canon, but they form a long section in the book of Jeremiah, and they are indispensable to his message. If the Christian preacher would claim any part of Jeremiah for a text, then he or she must be willing to hear the whole.

To be sure, the message of these oracles is frightful. Jeremiah is above all else here a prophet who hears sounds, and the Hebrew word for "sound" or "voice" permeates these passages. Just as in the initial vision of 1:13–15 (see above) the prophet "saw" a boiling pot, with its evil brew spilling out of the north toward the south, so he now hears that evil from the north let loose (4:15–16; see 10:22): the war-trumpet resounding throughout Judah (4:5; 6:1); Judah's populace crying out in alarm (4:5; 8:19) and urging flight before the enemy (4:5–6; 8:14); the generals in the foe's camp plotting their attack (6:4–5) in a strange tongue incomprehensible to the Judeans (5:15), followed by the snorting of the foe's stallions (8:16) and the roaring of their horsemen and archers, like the roaring of a great sea-wave (6:23; see 4:29), as they engulf Judah suddenly and swiftly (6:26). Then Jeremiah hears further sounds: of Zion crying out in distress like a woman in travail—panting, gasping, wailing "Woe!" as her land is laid waste (4:31); calling out for help from God or king (8:19) as she gives up her life (4:31; see 6:24; 8:20). And in reaction, the prophet himself hears the pounding of his own heart (4:19), and asks how long he must hear the blast of the *shophar* or war-trumpet in his ears (4:21).

But in these oracles the prophet also sees the coming destruction of his people: the foe roused up from the north like a lion from his lair (4:7); the war standard raised over Judah (4:6), and the people fleeing into the surrounding forests and rocky ravines of the Jordan valley (4:29); the swift chariots and horsemen of the enemy (4:13), their swords (6:25) and bows and spears (6:23); their siege mounds cast up against the walls of Jerusalem (6:3, 6); their cruel lack of mercy

(6:23); and then their total devastation of the land, its produce, its fortifications, and its populace (5:17; 8:16). These foes, says the prophet, are like poisonous snakes let loose among his people: there is no defense against their bite of death (8:17). So horrified is Jeremiah by this revelation of Judah's coming destruction that he cries out in agony to ask how long he must see in prophetic vision the war standard raised and the curtained walls of his own tents destroyed (4:20–21).

Indeed, so overwhelming is this vision of the future for the prophet that he likens it to a reversal of God's very creative act (4:23–26): The earth has returned to its original state of chaos (4:23; see Gen 1:2), in which God has taken back his light (4:23; see Gen 1:3) and removed the foundations of the earth (4:24; see Ps 104:5) and done away with creatures and human beings (4:25; see Gen 1:20, 26–31) and made the fruitful earth a desert once more (4:26; see Gen 2:5).

None of these oracles on the Foe from the North identifies that enemy. Earlier, many scholars thought the foe was the Scythians, a barbaric tribe from the Caucasus. Others have said that the foe is clearly the Babylonians, redating Jeremiah's oracles accordingly, while some have seen here an announcement of the coming Day of the Lord or even an ancient mythical account of the destruction of the world. But Jeremiah does not name this foe, and it is clear that the foe is a portrayal of God's wrath against his sinful people (4:8, 26). God rouses up this enemy. In short, God declares war against his covenant people (see Jer 1:4–10 and the end of the "warfare" in Isa 40:2). The Word laid upon the prophet's heart (4:19; 8:18, 21) by the Lord is a Word of war against Judah, whose death foreseen in these oracles is God's active and actual judgment upon her.

These oracles are intended only as warnings for Judah, however—portrayals of what may come upon her if she does not change her ways. Judah is sinful in God's sight in the very core of her being. Her "heart" is wicked; evil thoughts have taken up lodging within her (4:14), and evil ways dominate her actions (4:18). She trusts in everything but her God—in her own ability to save herself (4:30); in her fortifications (5:17) and her graven images (8:19). She practices violence and oppression with her society (6:6–7). She is wise in doing evil, but does not know how to do good (4:22). Therefore when God looks for healing and repentance and wholeness within her, he finds only the terror caused by sin within her society. And all of that is, Jeremiah holds, the sickness of Judah's "heart" (see 4:4; 17:1).

The prophets of Israel—Jeremiah among them—share with our Lord (see Mark 7:21–23) the conviction that sin is, at its core, a corruption of the inner person. It is in the very depths of our lives and loves that faithfulness to God must be formed, in a trust that will cling to him and obey his Word, come what may. Jeremiah, preaching as he is in this period shortly after the Deuteronomic reform, is calling his people to the love and fealty to God which Deuteronomy also sees as basic—the love of God with all one's heart and soul and might (Deut 6:5; see Mark 12:30 and parallels)—daily, constant, and reverent service of him in obedience and gratitude (Deut 10:12–13). That is what Jeremiah means by "good" (4:22; 6:16), and such a trusting life brings from God's hand "good" in return (Jer 5:25; Deut 30:15). But the basis of that "good" is total dependence on the Lord—trust in him for life and wisdom and righteousness and sanctification and redemption (1 Cor 1:30).

It follows that Jeremiah is dealing not only with social sins in Judah—not just with the oppression and violence found in his society and in ours—but also with the sins of our wayward hearts: with our trust in our own abilities and talents and cleverness to secure our lives; with our thoughts that we are righteous and that these judgments do not pertain to us; with our vain attempts to amend our lives by outward ritual and inner self-resolve; with our false and secret promises that yes, someday we will be truly religious and read the Bible and practice prayer and do some outstanding Christian deed. And to it all, Jeremiah replies, "How long shall your evil thoughts lodge within you?" (4:14). As C. H. Spurgeon preached:

> ... you Christian people who are always on the verge of being splendid, you members of churches who are always going to be generous, who are quite certain that you shall be useful, only you never are, what profit has ever come to God or your-

self from this continued hesitation? (*The Treasury of the Bible*, vol. 4, p. 10).

These oracles on the Foe from the North attack our evil hearts and call us to that dependent trust on God's grace by which alone we may be saved and by which our lives are amended truly to do the good.

Can the modern preacher use such texts as these? Most do not, of course, because they do not believe that God wars against his covenant people in the church. But Jeremiah gives the lie to such distortions of God's character. God hates sin, and he will war against it and do it to death. That surely is part of the message of the cross, and Jeremiah's bloody pictures of Judah's destruction find their parallel in that bleeding figure on Golgotha. But we must not think that the death of Christ exempts us from God's crucifixion of us, if we then refuse to trust the grace that was offered by the death of our Lord. God offered life to Judah if she would trust him wholely, just as he offers life to us if we will trust his redemption of us in his Son. But rejecting that, we can expect nothing else than God's warfare against us. The choice between death or life through Jesus Christ at God's hands is a real choice that is often overlooked in our time, and thus the preaching of the gospel has lost its urgency in the Christian church. But "the wages of sin is death" (Rom 6:23)—our "anything goes" society needs to hear that again; and perhaps the use of one of these oracles on the Foe from the North can serve as the medium of the message.

God's warnings to Judah were enfleshed for her in the troops of Babylonia, but the modern preacher will need to find analogies to the latter in our contemporary world. How does God work out his "temporal judgments," as the Westminster Confession calls them, in our place and time? Through warfare? Through the rise and fall of nations? The dis-ease of our anxious hearts? The breakup of families? The breakdown of communities under crime and injustice and bureaucratic bungling? Through venereal epidemics and drug trafficking and child abuse and neglect? Such evils threaten our lives as surely as Babylonia threatened Judah's. And are these God "giving us over" to our sin, as Paul would put it (Rom 1:24–32), as his judgments on our faithlessness? This God of the

Bible always has a hand in our world and must ever be seen at work in it.

The preacher probably should select only one of these oracles on the Foe from the North to use as a specific text for a sermon—perhaps 4:13–18, which includes so many of the central themes. The specific passage can then be put in its context in Jeremiah's book and also paired with a NT passage.

None Is Righteous (5:1–9)

This poem leads the list of those oracles that Jeremiah proclaimed during the period from 622 to 609 B.C., following the Deuteronomic reform under King Josiah. There are multiple indications in the book of Jeremiah that the prophet not only supported the reform, but was an instigator of it (see the section on Jeremiah and the Deuteronomic Reform, p. 00), in the hope that his people would repent and return to their God and thus avoid the coming judgment. But this oracle shows how vain was such a hope.

Jeremiah is commanded here (vs. 1), in a series of urgent imperatives ("run," "look," "take note," "search"), to peer into every nook and cranny of Jerusalem in the hope of finding one person who seeks to be faithful to the Lord (seeks "truth"; Hebrew: 'emunah), who walks in God's way (vss. 4–5), or who lives in the manner required by God ("does "justice," v. 1; Hebrew: mishpat). If Jeremiah can find such a person, God will forgive Judah her iniquity and turn aside the coming judgment.

There are few stronger proclamations of the mercy of God. God is willing to forgive a whole people for the sake of one righteous person among them—a willingness reminiscent of Gen 18:22–33; Isa 53:11; and above all, Rom 5:18–19—and the fact that this merciful invitation occurs in the midst of the oracles on the Foe from the North shows God's reluctance to destroy his chosen folk.

Unfortunately, Jeremiah's search is fruitless. The people break the third commandment of the Decalogue by taking oaths in the name of the Lord, even though they really do not believe God exists or acts (vs. 2; see vs. 12). They do not believe God will punish them, and they feel free to break their word. Indeed, the people ignore God's law embodied in the teachings of Deuteronomy, and the reform movement has had no effect on their daily walk (vss. 4–5; note that human life is a walk along a way, a constant movement forward toward a goal). Or, changing the figure, the people have totally shed the yoke of the torah by which God would guide them and give them life (vs. 5; see 2:20).

Further, the people will accept no correction of their ways (vs. 3). God has repeatedly tried to warn and correct them through historical and natural afflictions (vs. 3; see 2:30; 3:3; 31:18–19; Amos 4:6), but his message has been lost on foolish sinners, who have eyes but do not see and ears but do not hear (vss. 3–4; see vs. 21). They have steadfastly set their faces like a rock (see Luke 9:51) in the evil direction they are going, and they will not turn around to walk in God's direction (vs. 3). God's judgment on them, with its resulting death, is therefore inevitable (vs. 6). There is no pardon possible for deliberate idolatry, with its baalistic sacred prostitution (vs. 7), just as there is no pardon possible for the violation of community forbidden in the Decalogue's prohibition against adultery (vs. 8). If God is ever to bring in his good order, he must do away with the old (which is the force of "avenge" in vs. 9).

The remarkable fact in this oracle is that poor and rich alike are guilty. Jeremiah's initial search takes him among the poor—the beggars, the widows and orphans, but also the strangers and petty shopkeepers and tradesmen in Jerusalem's streets—the little guys, struggling to keep their heads above water, as they are buffeted by the powers that be. Jeremiah is very willing to give them the benefit of the doubt: they do not have the background, the education and money and status that would help them live righteous lives. But that is no excuse. "All alike" have broken the yoke—poor and rich, oppressed and oppressor, male and female, of whatever class. "None is righteous, no, not one" (Rom 3:10), and it is quite evident that the Bible's well-known partiality in favor of the poor (see Jer 5:27–28) nevertheless does not excuse the latter their faithless breach of covenant law. God demands faithful hearts and transformed lives, from rich and poor alike, a fact that organizations such as the Salvation Army have long recognized, but that has often been forgotten in some forms of liberation theology.

Slaves to Sin (6:9–12)

This oracle is a dialogue in three stanzas between God and his prophet (vss. 9, 10–11a, 11b–12), with the prophet speaking in the first and third stanzas, God in the second. It dates, like 5:1–9, from 622–609 B.C. and bears similarities with that poem, although it probably was spoken somewhat later in that period of reform. It is framed by the word "hand" (vss. 9, 12).

Once again God's mercy is illumined. In vs. 9, he bids the prophet examine every twig of Judah, the "remnant" of the vine of Israel left after the fall of the Northern Kingdom (see Isa 5:1–7; Ps 80:8–11), in the hope of finding at least one good grape (see 8:13) that will justify God's sparing the vine and not pulling it up and destroying it (see 1:10; Matt 15:13; John 15:2).

Jeremiah replies that his search is fruitless and his warnings to the people in vain. No one will listen to him (see 6:17; 7:13, 24–26, 28). Like their hearts (4:4; 9:26; see 5:23; 6:28; 7:24), the people's ears are "uncircumcised" (RSV margin, vs. 10; see Acts 7:51), that is, there is a film over them, a foreskin, so that they cannot hear. It is not only that they will not hear but also that they cannot hear (see Hos 5:4). Sin has so stopped their ears that the Word of God, meant to be a merciful gift of sustenance and guidance (see Deut 4:5–8), has become instead an object of distaste and disgust ("scorn," vs. 10), useless to prompt their repentance.

It is a vivid picture of the power of sin, which so captures and imprisons and stupefies, that it becomes impossible for a transgressing people to break free of its bonds and return to God's way. "Slaves of sin," Paul terms such a condition (Rom 6:16–18), and it is obvious from both Jeremiah and Paul that such slavery cannot be ended except by an act of God's that breaks the shackles of slavery, or opens the ears, or circumcises the hearts, or sets the captives free to return home to the Father. Until such freedom is given, the Word of God is heard by sinners as sheer folly (1 Cor 1:18–31), as shameful and disgusting (Jer 6:10), to be ignored or scorned in the world (see 5:13; 6:17, 19) as wholly unprofitable. Certainly such has often been the reaction to the proclamation of the Word of God.

Jeremiah, confronting the people's slavery to sin, is therefore bidden by God to pour out on them the deserved Word of judgment—a Word postponed (see Ezek 12:28) while the prophet searched for one good "grape" on the "vine," but a Word burning in Jeremiah's bones that he was weary of containing (see 20:9). Now God commands him to let loose the Word that it may work its destruction. The Word of God is active, effective force, according to the Bible. What the prophet speaks will be done. And all in Judah will be destroyed by God's judging hand that is stretched out against them (vss. 11b–12). Though slaves to sin, we nevertheless are responsible for our fall into slavery, and God will judge us because of the evil master we have chosen to serve.

Refuse Silver (6:27–30)

In the period following the Deuteronomic reform, Jeremiah used three different figures to portray God's persistent and merciful effort to find at least one faithful person in Judah who would justify God's sparing the nation from destruction. In 5:1–9, the prophet searches the streets of Jerusalem. In 6:9–12, he is a gleaner, looking for one good grape. Here he is an assayer or tester of metals, examining Judah for purity. But there is none to be found. Judah's "bronze," "iron" (vs. 28), and "silver" (vs. 30)—(the preacher should not allegorically equate these designations with particular groups in Judah)—are so shot through with impurties and dross that they are useless for God's purposes. No matter how much God has tried to refine them in the fires of various experiences, they remain "rebels," "slanderers" (see 9:4–5), "corrupters" (6:28). Their wickedness cannot be removed (vs. 29). Therefore the Lord rejects them as his people chosen to serve his purpose (vs. 30).

The covenant relation between God and Israel was a gift of pure grace, established by God long before Israel had done anything to deserve it (see Exod 19:4; Deut 7:6–8; Rom 5:6) and preserved by God's constant willingness to love and forgive. But God called Israel into the covenant relation with himself that he might use her as the means of bestowing his blessing on all the families of the earth (Gen 12:3)—that Israel might be a "kingdom of priests," mediating the knowledge of God to the rest of the world (Exod 19:6), that she might declare the wonderful deeds of him who called her out of darkness into his marvelous light (see 1 Peter 2:9), and thus draw all peoples into her fellowship, under the lordship of God. But as this passage makes so clear, God can use his chosen people for that purpose—in Israel and in the new Israel of the church—only if there is some purity in the people in the form of a willingness to obey God's covenant commandments (see Exod 19:5–6), which are preserved for us now in the Scriptures. Church people talk very glibly about God working through them, and heaven knows, God has worked through the most inadequate and sinful human instruments in the past. But this passage in Jeremiah raises a pertinent question: is there enough purity of obedience in us to make us useful for God's purpose, or are we so shot through with disobedience that God must simply reject us as his instruments and create others (see Exod 32:9–10; Matt 7:19)?

The Temple Sermon (7:1–15; 26:1–24)

Few passages are more relevant to our time than is this famous Temple Sermon of Jeremiah's, delivered in the gate to the outer court of the Jerusalem temple in 608 B.C., probably as pilgrims were thronging to that court during one of the three annual pilgrimage feasts (Tabernacles, Passover, or Weeks). The sermon is summarized by Jeremiah's scribe, Baruch, in 26:1–6 and the reaction of the populace to it recorded in 26:7–24. Thus, though the sermon is replete with Deuteronomic language, its content and context are well attested.

The sermon is first of all a call to amendment of life (vss. 5–7)—to the practice of justice within society in accordance with God's commandments; to the exercise of mercy toward the helpless; and to the relinquishment of all idolatry—all basic requirements found in the teachings of Deuteronomy, the covenant law of the land in the time of Jeremiah, and all frequently found in the teachings of the NT. The promise is that if the Judeans will fulfill such covenant requirements, they will be allowed to remain in Palestine—again a condition found frequently in Deuteronomy.

This call to a changed life comes, however, at the end of that period when it has become clear to God and his prophet that the Deuteronomic reform has failed. The call for repentance, therefore, serves more as a reminder of the conditions of the Deuteronomic covenant than it does as evidence of any hope on God's part that his people will change their ways. And indeed, the condition of the people is vividly set forth: They break the most basic of God's commandments, namely the Decalogue (the first, third, sixth, seventh, and eighth commandments are mentioned in vs. 9). The reader must recognize that the Ten Commandments were absolutely imperative for God's people, for apart from obedience to them Israel could not be a community, much less God's people (see Hos 1:9; 4:2—the only other passage in the prophets where the Decalogue is cited). Thus, Judah's disobedience has undermined the very foundations of her life.

Yet, because the temple stands there on Zion's hill, and because God has promised that he will place his "name" there (vss. 11, 12; see Deut 12:5 et passim)—that is, be present to his people—the Judeans think the temple is a magical guarantee that God will always do them good. They repeat, "This is the temple of the Lord" (vs. 4, see vs. 8), like some magical incantation that wards off all evil. They break the commandments and then go into worship and assure themselves that they are accepted by God and secure, only to leave the place of worship to break the commandments once again (vss. 9–10). In short, they turn the temple into a "den of robbers"— that is, a hiding place—where they are sure that God protects them, no matter what they do (vs. 11; see Jesus' use of the thought in Mark 11:17 and parallels). And just in case the Judeans think God is not aware of their smug assumptions and doings, he says in vs. 11b "Even I! Behold! I see!"

The sermon ends, therefore, in absolute judgment: the temple will be destroyed, as the central shrine of the tribal federation at Shiloh was destroyed by the Philistines in 1050 B.C., and the Judeans will be cast out of God's sight, off the land (see vss. 3, 14), into exile as northern Israel was exiled (vs. 15), in fulfillment of Deuteronomy's promise (see Deut 30:17–20).

According to Jer 26:7–24, the reaction to the prophet's sermon was swift. The priests and prophets and common people laid hold of him, the princes or leaders were summoned to the gate of the temple, and Jeremiah was accused of being a false prophet—a capital offense (see Deut 18:20). The charge was made on the basis of earlier prophetic predictions of the indestructibility of Zion (see Isa 31:4–5; 37:33–35) and of the promise to David (see 2 Sam 23:5). Jeremiah offered no defense other than to say that he truly spoke God's Word and that his accusers would be guilty of murdering an innocent man—again a capital offense (see Num 35:33)—if they put him to death (Jer 26:12–15). The princes and people therefore pronounced the prophet innocent (vs. 16). However, judging by vs. 24, the priests and prophets still threatened to lynch Jeremiah, despite an elder's reminder that Micah too, a century earlier, had predicted the destruction of Zion (vss. 17–19; see Mic 3:12. Verses 20–23 are an interruption inserted by Baruch and recount the death of another prophet). Jeremiah was saved from the lynch mob only by the intervention of Ahikam, a member of the reform group and an influential leader in the community (vs. 24; see 2 Kings 22:12, 14; 25:22), although the priests retaliated by henceforth barring Jeremiah from the temple (see 36:5). From this point on, Jeremiah was in danger of his life in Jerusalem, as Jesus was when he quoted Jer 7:11 at the cleansing of the temple (Mark 11:18).

What is there about this Temple Sermon that can arouse its hearers to such fury? It is not just that the sermon threatens the hearers with death—everyone from environmentalists to nuclear physicists makes such threats in our time. Nor is it that the people are charged with phony piety, in which their religiosity does not square with their evil deeds—even political candidates have made such charges against their opponents in recent times. No, the threatening aspect of this Temple Sermon, that turned its hearers against Jeremiah and Jesus and that still can unsettle congregations in our day, is that this sermon calls into question our fundamental presuppositions about God. On the basis of earlier promises of God, Judah in Jeremiah's time was sure that he would always forgive her, just as we in our day, on the basis of the cross and resurrection, are sure that God will always forgive us. And so we steal, in a hundred different petty ways; murder by automobile after Happy Hours and parties; commit adultery in blithe disregard of marriage vows; swear falsely to strike a plea bargain or to protect a reputation; covet the Joneses' standard of living or the latest fashion and fad; count aged parents useless to society; open the store seven days a week for the sake of profits; ignore the true nature of God; construct the image of God according to our own desires, and trust in every thing or any one but him. And then we go to worship on Sunday and believe "we are delivered," only to resume our breach of God's commandments early on Monday morning.

God is a forgiving and loving Father, we believe, who always accepts the sinner. Indeed, because we think he always loves and forgives, sin has lost its meaning for us. There is no offense, no matter how often repeated, which can separate us from his care. Such is the general view of God throughout the American public. Our religion has become for us a hiding place, a "den of robbers," assuring us of divine favor and protection no matter what we have done or left undone. This Temple Sermon of Jeremiah's affords the preacher the opportunity to challenge such attitudes, on the basis of the biblical witness.

Incomprehensible Sin (8:4–12)

This oracle serves as a good summary of Jeremiah's preaching during the years of 622–609 B.C., and it shows how futile were the efforts of the Deuteronomic reformers, including Jeremiah, to effect real change in the lives of the Judeans. Verses 10–12 are found also in 6:12–15, but they probably originally belonged here, the poem being bracketed by the word "fall" and by the oracular formulae in vss. 4 and 12. God speaks here, through Jeremiah's words.

The Lord begins this poem by citing familiar proverbs (vs. 4; see 2:32; 18:14), much like "What goes up must come down." The twist is that Judah does the unexpected. She has fallen and not risen, turned away and not returned. Rather, her "backsliding" from God's way is perpetual; her failure to return is deliberate and rebellious refusal; she literally clings ("holds fast") to deceit (vs. 5).

What "deceit" is involved? It is the "lie" of vs. 8, the false dealing of vs. 10—in short, the rejection of the Word of the Lord (vs. 9) and the refusal to know his true ordinance (vs. 7) or law (vs. 8). That ordinance and law, or better "teaching," has been set forth in the Deuteronomic covenant, accepted by King Josiah and the people (see 2 Kings 23:1–3; 2 Chron 34:29–33) and preached by Jeremiah (Jer 11:1–5, 6–8). But those responsible for teaching the people the torah—the priests and their scribes, the wisdom teachers and other prophets—have distorted the torah in their promulgation of it (see 5:31). As we are so often wont to do, they have softened God's demands ("one has to take account of mitigating circumstances"), bent and twisted them by reinterpretion ("it's the loving thing to do"), counted them fulfilled by the performance of empty ritual (see 6:20; 7:21–23), or turned them into irrelevant objects of esoteric scholarly discussion (see 9:23–24). At the same time, they tell the people "All is well" ("peace," vs. 11), in an ancient equivalent of "I'm O.K., you're O.K.," glossing over the people's sins and shortcomings in their relation with God.

The result is that no rein is laid upon the people's evil. When God listens for one word of repentance from his folk, no confession is heard (vs. 6). The people pursue their own ways, follow their own wills and desires, take the bit in their teeth and plunge headlong toward destruction—all of them greedy for wealth acquired unjustly, all of them defrauding the covenant (vs. 10).

Jeremiah understands the Deuteronomic torah here as a restraint on evil doings, much in the manner of Paul's view of the law in Gal 3:23. But it must be remembered that at the core of Deuteronomy is the call for love for God, which is then to be acted out in grateful obedience to his commandments (see John 14:15). And finally, here too, Jeremiah is calling for the repentance that comes from circumcised hearts and ears (see 4:4; 6:10, see RSV margin), and that leads to that faithful trust in God by which we are justified (Gal 3:24).

That Judah does not have such trustful and obedient love for her God is incomprehensible to Jeremiah (vs. 7; see 2:10–11, 31; 18:13–15). There is, however, in vs. 7, no thought of unseen spiritual laws automatically governing human life in a manner equivalent to what we call "natural law." The OT knows no law, natural or spiritual, that is divorced from God's direct action. God appoints and sustains the ways of nature (see Gen 8:22; Ps 104), as he appoints the way for Judah. But the dumb birds are wiser than God's foolish chosen people. They keep the migratory ways appointed for them, but Judah goes her own way (such is the meaning of vs. 7)— unashamed, unrepentant, and therefore unsaved. Judah will fall and never rise again in God's warfare against her (vs. 12; see vs. 4).

No Balm in Gilead (8:18–9:1)

This moving elegy, from which the familiar Negro spiritual, "There Is a Balm in Gilead," takes its metaphors (vs. 22), has been variously dated. Some place it in the period of 622–609 B.C. and maintain that it portrays the drastic drought that afflicted Judah in that period (see 14:1–10; 5:20–25; 18:13–17). Others date it about 600–598 B.C., at the beginning of the Babylonian invasion. Because of its present location, I am inclined to understand it as the portrayal of Jeremiah's reaction to the unrepentance of his people and to the inevitable doom that he has seen coming upon them in the form of the Foe from the North. In prophetic vision, Jeremiah has seen the ruin of his beloved people, just as Jesus foresaw the ruin of Jerusalem (Luke 19:41–44); and like Jesus, Jeremiah weeps. He hears in his ears the voices of the future—his people crying out for help (vs. 19ab), questioning why they are being destroyed, even though the Lord dwells in the temple in their midst (vs. 19cd), lamenting that the summer season—the time for military adventures—is over and no military ally has come to their aid (vs. 20). But he also hears God's justification for the wounding: the Judeans have grieved and provoked the Lord with their empty idols (vs. 19ef; the Hebrew recalls the uselessness of foreign gods, as in 2:4–13).

Here again are pictured those careless worshipers that we saw in 7:1–15, who believe that God in their midst will save them from harm no matter what they do. And when he does not turn aside their destruction, they blame him. They complain, but they do not repent. They are afraid, but they are not humbled before God. Instead, they believe that God owes them protection from trouble, because he has made a covenant with them. There is no recognition on the people's part of their covenant obligations of trust and obedience.

"We are not saved." No worse thing can be said of human beings, but not because salvation is a guarantee of freedom from trouble. That was Judah's problem—that that was the only kind of salvation she cared about. But not to be saved, in the Bible's understanding, is to lack room to live. The root meaning of the verb "to save" in the Hebrew is "to be capacious," "to be wide or spacious" (see the pictures in 2 Sam 22:20, 37; Pss 4:1; 31:8; Job 36:16; Isa 33:21). That room, that freedom, that lack of constriction are given only in the relationship with God, where the burdens of sin and guilt are lifted and the bonds of fear and anxiety are loosed and one has freedom to walk and breathe and become the person God intended. To be saved, in the Bible's thought, is to be brought into fellowship with the life-giving Lord and therefore to have the possibility of living abundantly. And given that possibility, then let the winter come with its storms and dark and cold; the saved face the worst and persevere in the strength of God's life and not in their own.

But if Judah wished to be saved from the winter that was coming, she had to circumcise her heart. She had to repent and give up her idols and trust in God alone. She had to have a new heart. And because she would not, Jeremiah is sick at heart (vs. 18). Is there no healing for this people, he cries, nothing to make them whole again? No ointment from Gilead's famous medicinal wares, no healing from any quarter? But Gilead's ointments could help heal wounds and cuts only of the body; Judah's sickness was of her heart. And so the prophet calls for a fountain of tears to express his anguish over the ruin that is coming on his compatriots.

This is a picture of what a true prophet feels about his sinful people—not anger, not scorn, but terrible, terrible grief— for the true prophet never separates himself from those to whom he preaches. Their suffering is his suffering, their ruin

his, their cries his weeping, their calls for help his petition,
even long before the people realize their desperate situation.
Indeed, as we shall see (see 16:1–9), the true prophet takes
within himself the judgment of God on his people and suffers
it first within his own body and soul. So it is that Jeremiah
weeps and is sick at heart.

The Weariness of God (9:2–9)

The key to understanding this poem is realizing that these
are words spoken by God, not only by his prophet. Commentators have often emended the word "me" in vss. 3 and 6 to
"the Lord," in order to make these Jeremiah's personal words.
But this is God's complaint—his reaction to all those sins of
Judah's through the years that Jeremiah has detailed thus far
in his book. William Cowper paraphrased this passage in a
poem about human weariness with evil:

> Oh for a lodge in some vast wilderness,
> Some boundless contiguity of shade,
> Where rumor of oppression and deceit,
> Of unsuccessful or successful war,
> Might never reach me more! My ear is pained,
> My soul is sick, with every day's report
> Of wrong and outrage with which earth is filled.

But if we have ever felt such weariness at the world's evil, how
much greater is the weariness of God! Here is the Lord who
is sorry that he has made humankind, who carries its sins like
a great burden on his grieving heart (see Gen 6:6), and who
therefore just wants to return to the desert from whence he
came (see Judg 5:4) and rent a room there, and abandon his
people once for all. It is a daring anthropomorphism. Judah
is threatened with God-forsakenness here, with the death
that comes from being without God in the world. The
preacher might contemplate just what such abandonment
would mean.

The reasons for God's heart-sick weariness are emphasized
in the "*ki*" phrases—those lines that begin in the English
translation with the word "for": all the Judeans are adulter-
ers against God's marriage covenant, an assembly of unfaithful ones (vs. 2e); all go from one evil to the next and know
nothing of God's character (vs. 3c); therefore, every brother

deceives his brother, as Jacob deceived Esau, and every friend goes about slandering his neighbor (vs. 4c).

"Knowledge of God" is a key concept in Jeremiah that signifies that inner, heartfelt intimacy with which a faithful wife knows her husband or an obedient son knows his father. To know God, according to Jeremiah, is to know his character, because one has lived day-by-day in his fellowship (9:24). It is to delight in his will (2:8; 4:22) and to follow his guidance (8:7) and to eschew every other lover (7:9; 10:14; 44:3). God knows Israel through and through (29:23), but she does not know him, treating him like a casual acquaintance unadmitted to her life and love. And so God is weary with his Judean bride (see 2:2) and tempted to give her up.

Judah's failure to know her God results in a corruption of her society that is portrayed here primarily as the corruption of speech and language (see Ps 12; Jas 3:1–12). No one speaks the truth (vss. 3, 5), and therefore no neighbor can trust another (vs. 4). One greets another with "*shalom*" ("peace") and yet inwardly is ready to bring him to ruin (vs. 8). Indeed, such deceivers prevail or are in charge of Judean society (vs. 3), and they not only will not reform (vs. 6), but also their lives are so tangled in a web of deceit that they have no power to break free of it (vs. 5).

The thoughtful preacher might ask what so corrupts the speech of a society. Certainly in a culture such as ours, where words are often intended to mean just the opposite of what they say; where "killing" can be termed "unlawful or arbitrary deprivation of life"; where few official announcements can be trusted to be the truth; and where even marriage partners draw up pre-nuptial contracts, we need to ask after the corruption of language. "Let what you say be simply 'Yes' or 'No'" Jesus said, without the necessity of oaths or contracts to confirm it; that is, let a person's word speak the truth (Matt 5:37). But where there is no responsibility felt to the truth of God, and where individuals and societies recognize no power beyond them, words become the instruments of self-aggrandizement, mirroring the deeper sinfulness of the heart.

Therefore, says the Lord in Jer 9:7, he will refine his people in the fires of judgment, melting out of them their impurities as one refines metal. The amazing fact in this verse, however,

is that God still names Judah "my people." He does not abandon them, as he would like to do. Rather, in great weariness
with their sin, but also in great patience, he takes upon himself the arduous task of trying to make them pure again. This
God never gives up, but labors further to transform his people
into the covenant society he wishes them to be.

The Necessity of the Judgment
(Jeremiah 9:17–25:13b)

Jeremiah and the Deuteronomic Reform
([6:16–19; 7:16–20, 21–34; 8:1–3];
11:1–17; 13:1–11; 14:11–16; 15:1–4; 16:10–13;
17:1–4; 18:1–12; 25:1–11a, 13ab).

It has long been recognized by scholars that there are in the book of Jeremiah extensive prose sections that resemble in style and content material in Deuteronomy and other Deuteronomic texts in various parts of the OT. Indeed, Sigmund Mowinckel isolated these prose passages and labeled them a separate source, including in the source Jer 7:1–8:3; 11:1–5, 9–14; 18:1–12; 21:1–10; 25:1–11a; much of chap. 32; 34:1–7, 8–22; 35:1–19, and 44:1–14. There has therefore been for years a debate among scholars as to how Jeremiah was related to the Deuteronomic reform that took place in 622/1 B.C. under the reign of Josiah of Judah (see 2 Kings 22:1–23:30; 2 Chron 34–35). Some scholars have denied that Jeremiah had anything to do with the reform, and most recently, Robert Carroll has maintained that the book of Jeremiah is largely a fiction put together by Deuteronomic redactors in the sixth century B.C. to show why Judah went into exile: Jeremiah symbolizes those true prophets to whom Judah should have listened. Such a position has not won many supporters.

To the contrary, there is much evidence to show that Jeremiah not only supported the Deuteronomic reform, but that he himself was a member of that reform party, which included those levitical priests that assembled the book of Deuteronomy. Jeremiah came in contact with such levitical reformers in his hometown of Anathoth in the territory of Benjamin, was himself the son of Hilkiah the levitical priest (1:1), and grew up in that priestly environment traced back to the priestly line of the Mushite Abiathar, to Eli and to the tribal sanctuary at Shiloh. His prophecies therefore show great sympathy for the northern forebear Rachel (31:15) and for the northern tribes (31:2–6, 7–9, 15–20, 21–22; 32:8, 44; 33:13; 50:17–28).

When Jeremiah's call came, it was a call to be "a prophet like Moses" (Deut 18:15), and it was framed in the language of the Holy War, so familiar from Deuteronomy (see my *Deuteronomy, Jeremiah*), just as Jeremiah's prophecies concerning the Foe from the North were framed in that language.

Further, Jeremiah's central requirement for the Judeans— that they write God's law on their hearts (31:33; 17:1)—parallels the thought of Deuteronomy (Deut 6:6; 11:18; 30:14). It was Deut 10:16 that Jeremiah quoted when he called for the circumcision of the heart (Jer 4:4; see 9:26), just as it was Deuteronomic requirement that the law be written on the heart which Jeremiah repeatedly said Judah never fulfilled (5:23; 9:14; 12:2; 13:10; see Deut 29:18; Jer 23:16–17, 26; 14:14). As in Deuteronomy, only love of God in the heart would bring "good" and "rest" (Jer 6:16; 32:39)—both key concepts in the book of Deuteronomy.

Jeremiah repeatedly called for obedience to the law of Deuteronomy (2:8; 6:19; see 18:18); he quoted Deut 15:1, 12 in 34:14, and Deut 21:14 in 34:16. His understanding of the nature of sin as consisting primarily in apostasy—false religious worship and practice—was the same as that found in Deuteronomy. He believed that the covenant curses of Deuteronomy had fallen on his sinful people because of their apostasy (compare 5:24; 14:22 with Deut 11:14; 28:12), and that they were a people who had eyes but did not see and ears but did not hear (5:21; Deut 29:4).

Finally, it was Deuteronomic reformers who afforded a hearing to Jeremiah's words (compare Jer 36:10–12 with 2 Kings 22:3, 8, 10, 12: Shaphan, Gemariah, Micaiah, Achbor). It was Ahikam, the son of Shaphan the reformer, who saved Jeremiah's life (26:24; see 2 Kings 22:12, 14), just as it was Shaphan's son Elasah who later acted as an agent for the prophet (29:3). The evidence for the connection of Jeremiah with the Deuteronomic reformers and their movement seems almost overwhelming, and we therefore are justified in interpreting the following passages in the context of that reform. Indeed, a number of other passages also belong in such context: 6:16–19; 7:16–20, 21–34; 8:1–3; 14:11–16; 15:1–4; 16:10–13; 17:1–4. All come from the period of 622–605 B.C., and I have included the discussion of them in the treatment of the three representative passages that follows.

Covenant Warning (11:1–17). This is probably the sole passage in Jeremiah's book in which he refers specifically to the covenant that Josiah made on the basis of Deuteronomy with the inhabitants of Judah in 621 B.C., although the "ancient paths" and "good way" of 6:16 are also a reference to that covenant law. Indeed, whenever Jeremiah speaks of the law and ordinances of God, he has Deuteronomy in mind.

There are in this passage most of the motifs found in Jeremiah's preaching of Deuteronomy: the call to hear and obey the covenant commandments (vss. 2, 6; see 6:16–17; 7:23; 18:11); the failure of Judah's forebears to heed God's persistent warnings by the prophets (6:17; 7:25; 25:4–7) and to be obedient (11:7–8, 10; 7:24–26; 16:11); the working out of the covenant curses and therefore the resulting judgment on those forebears, reaching its climax in the fall of the Northern Kingdom (11:8); the apostasy of Judah that is worse than that of even her forebears (11:13; 7:17–18, 30–31; 8:2; 13:10–11; 16:12; 17:2–3); the Lord's declaration of coming judgment on Judah (11:11, 17; 13:10; 16:18; 7:20, 32–34; 14:12, 15–16; 15:2–3; 16:13; 17:4); the inability of Judah's idols (11:12) and sacrifices (11:15; 7:21–22; 14:12) to prevent her doom.

There is also found in Jer 11:14 the admonition to the prophet not to intercede for his sinful people, and this is a frequent note in relation to his preaching of the Deuteronomic reform (see 7:16; 14:11). When Judah refused to listen to Jeremiah's words to turn away from her apostasy, God's judgment on her became inevitable, but the prophet in his love for his people nevertheless begged God to forgive them and to turn aside his wrath. God's reply was framed in questions to the prophet: "What right has my beloved in my house, when she has done vile deeds?" (11:15). "Do you not see what they are doing in the cities of Judah and in the streets of Jerusalem?" (7:17). In other words, God justified his judgment to the prophet by pointing to Judah's evil. She deserved to die. "The wages of sin is death." God's will cannot be successfully defied if he is in fact Lord of life. For our age, with its easy tolerance of wrong, that is a word to remember. Indeed, God told his prophet that even if Moses and Samuel, lawgiver and prophet, stood before him to intercede for Judah, he could not turn aside the doom that Judah had brought on herself (15:1). For according to 11:8, God's judgment was a working out of the covenant curses found in Deuteronomy, and God always kept his Word. He had promised life in the land if Judah loved and obeyed him, but death and expulsion from the land if she turned aside to other gods (see Deut 28; 30:15-20). The judgment that was coming was the evidence of God's faithfulness to his promises!

More than that, judgment on Judah is conceived by this prophet as the working out of Judah's own evil actions. In God's universe, according to much of the OT, evil returns upon its instigators (see 1 Kings 8:31-32). It works its own effects—not automatically, but because God wills such working. And so in 6:19, the judgment that the Lord is bringing on Judah is "the fruit of their devices;" in 7:19, it is "their own confusion;" in 14:16, it is their own wickedness. Sin against God returns upon the head of its perpetrator. "Whatever a man sows, that he will also reap" (Gal 6:7). There is no way, as the wicked hopes, that "God has forgotten, he has hidden his face, he will never see it" (Ps 10:11). Sin brings with it its own evil recompense for the sinner. These passages furnish the preacher a good opportunity to examine the consequences of evil doing, an examination rarely undertaken in our live-and-let-live society, where God is believed absent from the world and where we therefore no longer believe ourselves responsible to him for our beliefs and actions.

It is noteworthy in 11:14-17 that the judgment which God pronounces on Judah is not very specific, characterized only by the words "trouble," "doom," "tempest," "fire," and "evil." The particular nature of the judgment is not given, and this seems characteristic of Jeremiah's early preaching of the Deuteronomic reform (see 6:19). There is warning here, but no specific sentence pronounced. Indeed, as we shall see in the following passages, God held out to Judah through the prophet the gracious invitation to return to him. But when that invitation was refused, the judgment became very specific.

God the Potter (18:1–12). God is the Potter, we are the clay: the Bible is sure of that fact. Throughout its pages it pictures a transcendent, holy, almighty God, who is always other than his creation, but who has nevertheless stooped down to form from the mud of chaos' material all persons and things. His hands have shaped the earth (Isa 45:18; Jer 33:2) and formed the dry land (Ps 95:5). His fingers have lifted up the mountains (Amos 4:13) and curved the energy of light (Isa 45:7). Indeed, Isa 37:26 even pictures human history as a ball of clay that the Lord is molding in his hands (so a literal reading of the Hebrew text). But lest we think this Creator God is occupied only with large projects, his hands have also formed the locusts (Amos 7:1) and the rods and cones of the human eye (Ps 94:9). This God shaped the human body in the beginning (Gen 2:7; 1 Tim 2:13), just as he knit Job together with bones and sinews (Job 10:8–11) and formed Jeremiah in his mother's womb (Jer 1:5). And this potter God made the nation Israel (Isa 27:11; 43:1, 7, 21; 44:2, 24) to be his servant people (Isa 44:21; 49:5). Thus, God was the Creator of Israel and her Father (Isa 64:8), the one who brought her into being and for whose purposes she was made, and in that role Israel is representative of all persons and of all created things. "Thou hast made us for thyself, O Lord, and our hearts are restless until they find their rest in thee" (Augustine). This figure of the Potter in the Bible is expressive of the origin and purpose of all creation.

Since God is the Potter and we are the clay, it would not seem proper therefore for the clay to question or to resist what the Potter is doing with it. "Does the clay say to him who fashions it, 'What are you making'? or 'Your work has no handles'?" (Isa 45:9). "Who are you, a man, to answer back to God? Will what is molded say to its molder, 'Why have you made me thus?' Has the potter no right over the clay?" (Rom 9:20–21). Would the Potter not reply, to borrow from Jesus' parable, "Am I not allowed to do what I choose with what belongs to me?" (Matt 20:15). Who are we, mere lumps of dirt, to challenge him who fashions us? It is God alone who has brought us into being and even breathed his life-giving spirit into us (Zech 12:1). How, then, can we question God or resist what he is doing with us?

But God, it seems, values us more than mud—indeed more than anything else in all creation (see Matt 6:26, 30)—and far from manipulating our lives and history, he asks us to participate in his purpose and to give back to him the love with which he has so carefully and wonderfully made us (see Ps 139:13–18). The Potter lets human clay talk back to him, respond to him, love him! And with that gift, the Creator elevates us above all other works in his creation.

So here in Jer 18:1–12, God the Potter offers Judah her true glory—the opportunity to love her Maker as he has loved her in fashioning her for his purpose. In fact, that Potter is willing to forgive all her past recalcitrance, all her misshapen compromises of his purpose, all her stubborn opposition to his destiny for her. Time and time again the Potter has found the clay opposing him and has started over with it. Yet one more time he is willing to cancel the past and begin anew. He can make of Judah a glorious vessel for his purpose, if she will but let him do so, just as the Apostle Paul says God the Potter can form the very image of Christ in our clay, if we will but allow it (Gal 4:19; see 2 Cor 3:18). But Judah replies, "That is in vain! We will follow our own plans, and will every one act according to the stubbornness of his evil heart" (vs. 12). And so the misshapen vessel Judah will be broken, her pieces crushed and discarded by her Maker.

Judgment Specified (25:1–11a, 13ab)   This passage apparently earlier formed the conclusion to the original scroll of Jeremiah's prophecies, which was read before all the people and then before King Jehoiakim in 605 B.C. (see chap. 36). It is probable that the references to seventy years and to the punishment of Babylon (vss. 11b–12) and the reference to the nations (vs. 13c) were not a part of that scroll and that Jeremiah's prophecies were directed solely toward Judah at this time. His announcement, then, was that the Lord was bring-

ιe tribes of the north—that is, the Foe from the
_ .ɔw identified specifically as Babylonia—to war
against Judah for her sin, and that as a consequence, the land
would become "a ruin and a waste" (see 7:34).

For twenty-three years, Jeremiah had spoken and pleaded
with his apostate people to no avail (vs. 3). For centuries, God
had warned Israel through the words of his prophets not to
go after other gods, but Israel had not listened (vss. 4–7).
Therefore God's warfare against his people would come; they
would be utterly destroyed; and their destruction would
show to other nations that they had been cursed by their God
(vss. 8–9). In a picture original with him, Jeremiah says that
all the daily pleasantries and occupations of life will cease—
the grinding of meal and the lighting of lamps, marrying and
giving in marriage, enjoyments large and small (vs. 10; see
7:34; 16:9; Isa 24:8–11; 47:2; Rev 18:23). Judah will be left
desolate and joyless.

So the judgment has now become specific in contrast to the
general warning given in 11:1–17. The sword will come, accompanied by the hunger and pestilence that are companions
to siege (see 14:14–16) and Judah will be hurled from her
land (see 16:13) and go into captivity (see 13:10; 15:2; 17:4).

God wills life and good for his people, but those can be had
only in that relationship of trust and obedience that is required in the covenant bond. When the bond is broken by
apostasy and rebellion, death engulfs the land. "See, I have
set before you this day life and good, death and evil," announced Deuteronomy (30:15). Judah stands at the crossroad
of decision, and chooses her own ruin. Should not the new
covenant people, the church, remember that when they too
stand daily at the crossroad (see Matt 7:13–14)?

The Confessions of Jeremiah (11:18–23; 12:1–6; [13:20–27]; 15:10–11, 15–21; [16:1–9]; 17:14–18; 18:19–23; 20:7–13, 14–18).

These passages in the book of Jeremiah have long been
termed his "confessions," because all are intimate prayers directed to God, with the exception of 20:14–18, which is a
curse. However, from the standpoint of form criticism, all of

these prayers, again with the exception of 20:14–18, are individual laments, whose structure is well known to us from the Psalms. Their typical form includes an invocation to God, followed by a complaint describing the prophet's desperate situation, a petition for aid, and an expression of certainty that God has heard the prayer.

Because of this similarity with individual laments in other parts of the OT, some scholars have held that these prayers are not original with Jeremiah and that they cannot be used to construct his biography. Yet the standard lament form is used rather freely in these prayers. Sometimes the order of its parts is changed (15:15–21; 20:7–13). Sometimes the certainty of a hearing is replaced by an oracle of judgment on the prophet's foes (11:21–23), by a warning to the prophet (12:5–6), by a call to the prophet to repent (15:19), or by the omission of any answering Word from God (18:18–23). In short, the original cultic form of the lament has been adapted to Jeremiah's circumstances, and these passages have about them the ring of authenticity. It would not be unusual for one from a priestly house to use cultic forms. And it also should not be surprising to find God directly addressing his prophet at prayer.

Several prose passages have been attached to these confessions to explain their occasion and some of their content. 16:1–9 explains the meaning of 15:17. 18:18 gives the occasion for 18:19–23, and 19:1–20:6 connects 20:7–13 with a particular sermon and with a particular instance of suffering on the part of the prophet. But the confessions themselves furnish the best clues to their occasions, and it is important for the preacher to understand these.

First, it seems clear from 12:1–6 and 11:18–23 (which should be read in that order) that Jeremiah's initial preaching in his hometown of Anathoth against the false piety (12:2) of his friends and neighbors and, apparently, of even his own family (12:6) led them to plot against his life (11:19). In his youthful naivete, Jeremiah was unaware of the plot (11:19), but was warned of it by the Lord (12:6; 11:18), whereupon the prophet fled his hometown and went to Jerusalem (12:5), the site of most of his preaching. At this time, Jeremiah ap-

parently had full confidence in God's protection of him
(11:20), despite the fact that a break with family and friends
certainly caused him grief.

When his preaching of the Deuteronomic reform occa-
sioned no repentance on the part of his sinful countrymen,
Jeremiah therefore faithfully poured out the words of judgment upon Judah that his Lord put within his mouth.

In 609 B.C., King Josiah was killed at the battle of Megiddo
while trying to halt the Egyptian march northward. His son
Jehoahaz followed him on the throne, but Neco II of Egypt
quickly deposed Jehoahaz and replaced him with the vassal
Jehoiakim. Egypt could hold sway for only four years, however. Nebuchadnezzar crushed Egyptian power (Jer 46:3–12,
14–24), assumed the Babylonian throne, and marched south
into Syria and Palestine. By the end of 604, he was in the
Philistine plain (Jer 47:2–7), where he destroyed Ashkelon,
and by 603/2, Jehoiakim had become his vassal (2 Kings 24:1).
The Foe from the North was now obviously to be identified
with Babylonia, and Jeremiah announced that doom was at
hand.

Two passages especially set forth the inevitability of that
doom. The first is 13:20–27, where Jeremiah employs a prov-
erb to portray the ineradicable nature of Judah's sin: "Can the
Ethiopian change his skin/or the leopard his spots?/Then also
you can do good/who are accustomed to do evil" (vs. 23). Judah could not change her ways, and so Jeremiah pronounced
her death: "Woe to you, O Jerusalem" (vs. 27). Her sin had to
be cleansed from her by the fire of judgment.

Further, according to the second passage, Jeremiah himself
became the living symbol of that judgment (16:1–9). He was
forbidden by God to attend a funeral or a party or a wedding,
just as earlier he had been forbidden marriage and offspring.
Jeremiah could have no heir to perpetuate his name—the
only form of immortality known to the Hebrews at the time—
and that was prophetic symbol of the fact that the heirs of
Judah would also die (vss. 1–4). But Jeremiah also could not
engage in the communal activities of mourning and feasting
and celebrating (vss. 5–9), because all those acts were gracious gifts of a gracious God, and now God was withdrawing
all grace—all covenant love, all tender mercy (vs. 5)—from

his apostate people. It is a gift of God, the passage implies, to be able to weep or to rejoice together (a marvelous view of a funeral!), and God was withdrawing his merciful gifts to his people. Jeremiah sat alone, as prophetic symbol of that fact, his only companion his scribe Baruch, and his only joy his service for God.

But for three years, from 604–601 B.C., the Babylonians did not attack Judah, and the judgment announced by Jeremiah did not come. That was the occasion for Jeremiah's confessions. In them, we see him wrestling with this apparent failure of the Word of the Lord. His compatriots hooted at him, "Where is the word of the Lord? Let it come!" (17:15). They accused him of being a false prophet (20:10). They cursed him and openly opposed him (15:10), mimicking his words (20:10) and even once subjecting him to beating, arrest, and a night in the stocks, where every passerby could hit him and spit on him (20:1–2). In such a situation of persecution, Jeremiah was totally dependent on the presence and sustaining power of God. He was set against the whole land, as promised in 1:18–19, and his only succor was his Lord. What, then, if that Lord should prove untrue? That is the terror with which the prophet wrestles in these laments.

Will God Prove True? (15:10–11, 15–21). Chronologically, this may be the last of Jeremiah's confessions, because it shows the prophet at the extremity of his suffering, not only threatened by all around him, and not only questioning his role as a prophet, but also doubting the faithfulness of his God and therefore in danger of losing both his prophetic office and his relationship with the Lord. Both his faith and his call to prophetic office must therefore be renewed. Verses 12–14 are probably misplaced from 17:3–4, and vs. 15a, which reads simply "you know" in the Hebrew, forms the final part of vs. 11. The address, "O Lord," belongs at the beginning of vs. 15b.

The prophet bemoans his birth to a prophetic calling that demands that he constantly defend himself against the accusations of his compatriots (vs. 10). "Strife" and "contention" are legal terms, and Jeremiah feels himself on trial for his life. He has never rejected his people (probably the meaning of "lent"), and yet they have rejected him. Indeed, the prophet has constantly interceded before God to turn aside the judgment on his sinful people. If that is not so, prays Jeremiah, then let the curses they have uttered against him be effected (vs. 11).

But there is only one way this prophet can be vindicated in the eyes of his compatriots—by the fulfillment of the words of judgment that he has pronounced against Judah. Only that fulfillment will show him truly to be a prophet from God. Jeremiah therefore prays that the Lord will not be forbearing against his people, that is, that the Lord will not go on forgiving Judah so long that Jeremiah's words of judgment turn out to be empty threats (vs. 15). If that should happen, then Jeremiah could be executed as a false prophet (see Deut 18:20–22).

That is a terrible request on the part of one who has never desired the destruction of Judah. Time and again Jeremiah has interceded on Judah's behalf (7:16; 11:14; 14:11). Time and again he has pleaded with his sinful compatriots to mend their ways. Time and again he has wept over the destruction he has foreseen to be coming upon them. He has even tried to shut up God's Word of judgment inside him and not to preach it (20:9), but all has been in vain. So now here, pushed to the limit, his life in the balance, Jeremiah begs for the promised judgment to come. There is no other way out for sinful Judah, and there is no other way out for endangered Jeremiah. But he is terribly, terribly afraid that God will show mercy after all (see Jonah 4:1–3).

Jeremiah therefore recounts the suffering he has endured in his task of proclaiming the judgment (vs. 17). God's hand has been upon him, that is, he has received the revelation of God's Word in some sort of prophetic, ecstatic experience and, as symbol of the content of that Word of judgment, Jeremiah has sat alone—forbidden to marry, to have a son, to attend a funeral, a party or a wedding (16:1–9). Yet, God's words to him and God's presence with him have given him joy also (15:16). He has "eaten" God's words, that is, they have come from outside of him and have been taken into his inward parts (see Ezek 2:8; 3:3; John 4:31–34; Rev 10:9–10) and laid upon his heart. That intimate communion of obedience, in which God's name has been called over him and in which he has belonged to God and God has belonged to him, has caused him the greatest joy.

But now, in the depth of despair and fear, Jeremiah questions God's faithfulness. Has God called him into intimate fellowship, only to desert him at the last? Has God given him words to proclaim that never will find fulfillment? Will God, "the fountain of living waters" (2:13), prove to be a "deceitful brook" after all (15:18), that is, like one of those dry wadis in the desert that run full after a rain, but that dry up immediately when the sun beats down (see Job 6:15–20)?

Jeremiah is one here with every person who has lived in intimate fellowship with God and who, in the midst of danger or dispute, has taken a stand on the Word of God. He is one with Moses, defying an empire on the basis of that Word; one with Elijah, challenging a queen; one with Daniel, facing the lions; one with Luther, defying pope and electors; just as he is also one with a Bonhoeffer, saying no to a Hitler, and a Martin Luther King, Jr., challenging a nation. But he is also one with every ordinary Christian, who has ever dared to defy society's convention and powers in the belief that the Word of God is true and that God's way and God's will shall finally triumph. Faithful souls stake their lives, their fortunes, their sacred honor on the belief that God will be true to his Word. But what if God proves not true? What if the Word is a lie and God will not fulfill it after all? What if the fountain of living waters is instead a temporary freshet that will dry up in the heat of the day? Is that not finally the question our Lord asked when he cried out from the cross, "My God, my God, why have you forsaken me?" "Wilt thou be to me like a deceitful brook, like waters that fail"?

The answer that Jeremiah received is an answer for every Christian, for first it rebukes our desperate temptations to lose heart and trust when we face adversity or when God seems to be doing nothing at all. "If you return, I will restore you" (vs. 19). In short, it is never God who is faithless, but we ourselves, and though heaven and earth should pass away, his Word will not pass away. God can be trusted to keep his promises, though all the evidence seem contrary. Christian faith can always take its stand confidently upon the Word of God.

It is, however, that Word alone to which faith is to cling. "They shall turn to you, but you shall not turn to them" (vs. 19), Jeremiah is told. Put another way, make no compromises with the Word. Do not give in to society's ways and easy accommodations. Cleave to the Word with all your heart, in the trust that it will be fulfilled.

Second, Jeremiah is told that if he repents and trusts his Lord once again, God will be with him to save and to deliver him (vs. 20). Those are the same words that Jeremiah heard at the time of his initial call (1:8, 19). The prophet is reinstated in his prophetic office. Despite his doubt and complaints, indeed, despite his blatant blasphemy of accusing God of duplicity, Jeremiah is forgiven and restored to God's presence and allowed to work for God's purpose once more. God does not throw us away when our faith fails. He grants us the mercy that allows us to repent and cling to his Word once again. Perhaps that is the final meaning of Christ's cry of dereliction from the cross—that he does not reject us in our doubt and weakness, but takes even that upon himself, and suffers our faithlessness for us, that we may be redeemed out of that final failure also.

God the Seducer and Warrior (20:7-13). In its present location, this confession follows immediately on the account of Jeremiah's action of breaking the potter's flask in the valley of Topheth, as symbol of the breaking of the people and the city (19:1-13), his prophecy in the temple court announcing evil for all Judah (19:14-15), Pashhur the priest's overnight detention of Jeremiah in the stocks, and Jeremiah's subsequent prophecy against Pashhur (20:1-6). Thus, in its present context, the confession would seem to be Jeremiah's reaction to the experience of being literally a "laughingstock" (20:7). However, the passage may have been placed in its present location because of the catchword, "Terror on every side" in 20:3 and 20:10. As is plain from 17:14-18, the prophet has been bothered for some time by the scorn and mockery of his countrymen, who ridicule him because his prophecies of doom have not come to pass.

Few passages more clearly illustrate the suffering involved in living one's life in faithfulness to the Word of the Lord. Here there is no easy choice between God's Word and society's ways, no happiness and earthly success given for following the Word of God, no blissful contentment found in being the servant of the Lord. On the contrary, Jeremiah accuses God of seducing him (vs. 7). The verb (translated "deceived" in the RSV) is used in Exod 22:16 of the rape of a virgin, in 1 Kings 22:21–22 of the enticing of Ahab by a lying spirit, in Judg 16:5 of Delilah's seduction of Samson. God has enticed, seduced, tricked Jeremiah into surrendering to him, Jeremiah thinks. God has been stronger than the prophet and has prevailed against him, forcing him into a ministry that he had no desire to undertake, and demanding that he proclaim a Word that he has no wish to proclaim. As a result, Jeremiah has become an object of scorn and mockery continually. Every time he speaks, it is not good news he announces, but violence and destruction (vs. 8), and because that prophecy goes unfulfilled, he has become an object of derision every day and all day. Nor is there escape for Jeremiah from the situation. If he tries to shut up God's Word inside of him, it becomes like a fire burning in his bones, and he cannot contain it (vs. 9). He must preach, but that brings the opposition of even his familiar friends, who watch to see if they can condemn him as a false prophet and thus sentence him to death in accord with the law (vs. 10).

Such a pericope gives the lie to every promise that faithfulness to the Word of God brings with it only peace and joy, and surely the passage is a mirror of what such faithfulness has cost every servant of the gospel, just as finally it is a mirror of part of what it cost our Lord. We acclaim the heroes and martyrs of the faith without really realizing what they have endured, and this confession could be used by the preacher to illumine the sacrifice involved throughout the history of the church. Here, surely, are the words of the Suffering Servant or Paul, of Luther or Damien, of Bonhoeffer or Martin Luther King, Jr., as well as those of Jeremiah.

Here however are also the words of a free man—a paradoxical statement on the face of it. If any person is a slave to his Lord, it is this prophet. He is set under compulsion to announce Judah's destruction, and he cannot break free of that necessity. He might have paraphrased Paul, "Woe to me if I do not preach the [Word]" (1 Cor 9:16). And yet, note well, this prophet is slave neither to his sinful world nor to his sinful self. He lives in the world but is not of it. Rather, he has his life totally from the hand of God, and that God is faithful and good and is working out a purpose of salvation. Jeremiah therefore can rest his case with the Lord and praise God for a deliverance which the world can neither give nor ever take away (vss. 12–13).

Jeremiah describes the Lord, in whose presence he lives and trusts, as a "dread warrior" (vs. 11). We do not, in our time, characterize God in such terms, but it is a description of God's person essential to the biblical witness. Jeremiah's God is at war against Judah's sin, just as surely as he is also at war against ours. Jeremiah has heard the sounds and seen the sights of that coming war (see the section on the Foe from the North), and they are dreadful in their portent. Jeremiah knows, according to the words of this confession, that God's judgment on Judah will come and that therefore his preaching of doom will be vindicated, while those who scorn his message will be eternally dishonored, as they are at this day. God is not Lord unless he wars against human defiance of him, and he is not good except he be also an enemy of our evil. So over against all our attempts to have it our own way, over against every desire of ours to compromise his will, stands this dread Warrior God of this prophet in Judah.

Finally, this confession shows forth the power of the Word of God. It cannot be turned back as it works out God's purpose. It cannot be silenced, either by reluctant prophet or scornful opponent or, in our case, by doubting demurrer. It is like a fire that will burst out beyond every effort to contain it (vs. 9) and like a hammer that will shatter every rock that seeks to block its way (23:29). When that Word became flesh, death itself could not silence him, and the grave with its great stone door could not contain him. The Word of God, finally incarnate in Jesus Christ, is the supreme power at work in the world, and at the last, every knee shall bow and every tongue confess that he is Lord, to the glory of God the Father.

Why Was I Born? (20:14–18). The faith to which Jeremiah gave expression in 20:7–13 does not prevent him from being plunged into the depths of deepest despair, as we now see in this confession. To be sure, Jeremiah has not lost his trust that the "dread Warrior" of 20:11 is with him. Rather, it is precisely the presence of that divine Warrior in his life that occasions this curse. God destined Jeremiah from before his birth (1:5) to be a prophet, to announce the destruction of his sinful people. That mission is the sole reason Jeremiah was born and the whole purpose for which God called him into existence. And it is just that mission that the prophet here repudiates. He would rather not have lived than to have come into the world for such a reason. He would rather not have been born than to have been called to be God's prophet against Judah. As a result, he here curses the day on which he was born and the man who announced his birth.

This curse is not a prayer, as are the other confessions, but rather a form of speech known to all religions, in which reliance is placed entirely on the independent power of the spoken word. It is considered that once a curse is spoken, it becomes effective against its object. To be cursed means to be dead, to be stricken from existence, to be consigned to the realm of chaos and evil and death. Thus, when Jeremiah curses the day of his birth (see Job 3), he is saying, let that day disappear from the calendar, let it be blotted out of time, let history be reversed, so that he himself will never have been born on the day. Such a wish is the closest to suicide that a Hebrew could come, for self-destruction was very infrequent in ancient Israel. Because the Hebrews had no belief in an afterlife until the second century B.C., they had no thought that they could escape in death to something better. Jeremiah is rejecting here everything that he is, in an irrational attempt to alter time and thus not be, in some reshaped history.

He speaks of his mother in vs. 14 and mentions his father in vs. 15, but he never curses them. To do so would have been an unforgivable sin in Israel, and Jeremiah wishes neither to sin against his parents nor against his God. He does, however, curse the neighbor who took the tidings of his birth to his father. The greatest bitterness and sarcasm are evidenced in vs. 15 when Jeremiah thinks of the joy his birth brought to his father. The birth of a son was always the occasion for rejoicing in Israel, for the continuance of the family name in the son was the Hebrew's only form of immortality. Jeremiah therefore contemplates in utter distaste the joy of his father over his birth. With total irrationality, he asks that the well-meaning neighbor become like Sodom and Gomorrah (Gen 19:24-28)—paradigmatic examples of God's destruction (see Hos 11:8)—and that he hear a cry of alarm in the morning and the warning of invaders at noon. Why?—because the neighbor did not kill him in the body of his mother and let her womb be his grave. The neighbor could not have done such a thing of course without bringing blood guilt on himself, but Jeremiah's irrationality has reached its zenith here.

In short, Jeremiah here rejects the total purpose and task of his life, and he ends with a sob. The Hebrew of vs. 18 reads, "Why this? From the womb I came forth to see misery and grief, and my days are consumed in shame." Like Job, Jeremiah seeks some reason for his fate. Perhaps if he could understand why he has to go through such suffering, he would be able to accept it. But no answer is given him here. His life is simply one unrelenting pain, spent in shame that eats up all his days. He has been chosen for a mission he despises, whose outcome he cannot perceive, whose burden of grief and ridicule he cannot bear, and whose purpose he cannot finally fathom, and under the weight of such a calling, he collapses and wishes he were dead. Surely it is a picture of the prophet in the lowest depths of his despair.

It is, however, also a picture with which many persons in modern congregations can identify—the newly divorced for whom life has lost all reason; the man slowly wasting away from multiple sclerosis or cancer, who believes he is nothing but a burden to his family; the elderly woman with powers gone who states, "I don't know why I am here;" the soul overcome by the weight of trouble and suffering. All of them can ask, "Why this?" And countless persons even among the faithful have questioned, "Why was I ever born?"

The remarkable fact is, however, that Jeremiah recorded this passage for us and could look back on his own despair from the advantage of purpose regained. He was born for a mission—to be God's prophet to the nations—and God faithfully stood by him through that mission and brought it to its desired conclusion. So too each person in the Christian church is called into that Body of Christ for God's purpose, and God will not leave us until he has done for us all that he has spoken to us (Gen 28:15). Writes Paul, "I am sure that he who began a good work in you will bring it to completion at the day of Jesus Christ" (Phil 1:6). God brought his good work in Jeremiah to its completion. And so too will he complete in each one of us, despite any circumstance, the purpose for which he has called us.

The Hatred of God and the First Deportation (12:7–13)

In 601 B.C., the troops of Nebuchadnezzar of Babylon engaged the forces of Neco II of Egypt on the latter's frontier. Both sides suffered greatly in the battle, and Nebuchadnezzar returned home to spend the next year reorganizing his army. Encouraged by the withdrawal of this "Foe from the North," his vassal, Jehoiakim of Judah, revolted. For two years Nebuchadnezzar did not respond. He did however dispatch guerrilla bands of Arameans, Moabites, and Ammonites against Judah, and it is this situation that is reflected in these verses in chap. 12 (see 2 Kings 24:1–2).

Destroyers attack Judah from the western desert, like birds of prey falling on an injured bird or hyena (vs. 9 in Hebrew). They leave behind them great destruction, but their harassing raids are but prelude to the destruction that Jeremiah sees coming upon Judah. All the land will be made desolate by foreign kings ("shepherds," vs. 10), and no one in Judah will have *shalom* ("peace," vs. 12), because the swords of the enemies are but the instrument of God's devouring sword of judgment (vs. 12). For all their efforts at self-sufficiency, the Judeans will have no return for their labors (vs. 13). They cannot live when they defy their God (see vs. 8).

Most commentators have given scant notice to this passage in Jeremiah's book, but for the preacher, it is pregnant with possibilities. Here we find the chilling words that God hates his people (vs. 8). We do not discover such a thought often in the Scriptures. It is frequently said that human beings hate God (see Exod 20:5; Deut 7:10; 2 Chron 19:2, et al.), just as they hate his Son (see John 7:7; 15:18, 23–25). And there are a multitude of evils that the Lord hates: the worship of foreign gods (Deut 12:31; 16:22; Jer 44:4), workers of iniquity (Ps 5:5), those who love violence (Ps 11:5), insincere worship (Isa 1:14), robbery and wrong (Isa 61:8), haughty eyes, a lying tongue, and false witnesses (Prov 6:16–19; see Rev 2:6). In Deuteronomy, Israel mistakenly believes that it is because the Lord hates her that he has brought her out of Egypt into the wilderness (Deut 1:27; 9:28). And Job, just as mistakenly, believes that God hates him as an enemy (Job 16:9). But only in Amos 6:8 and Hos 9:15 do we find God hating a whole people, and even there it is the apostate Northern Kingdom. Yet now, here in Jeremiah, God plainly says of his beloved heritage (see Ps 94:5; Joel 2:17; Mic 7:14, 18), his chosen people, "I hate her" (Jer 12:8).

The preacher might ask what it would mean for the church if God hated us. Surely the glories of beauty and order in the natural world would not be there, for they have been made through the love that is Jesus Christ (John 1:3). The divine blessings that are the joys of family and the comforts of community would never be known, because they come from the hand of a God of love (see Pss 127; 133). Forgiveness would never be given for any dark act, healing never known for any affliction (see Ps 103). Wisdom, righteousness, sanctification, redemption—none would be possible (see 1 Cor 1:30). "Love, joy, peace, patience, kindness, goodness, faithfulness, gentleness, self-control" would never be granted by the Spirit (Gal 5:22–23). And the chaos that is human life forsaken by God would be stilled only by the grave's dark silence. We are indeed set before the choice of life or death, blessing or curse, in our relation with God. And we need to have pictured for us the difference between those alternatives. If God hates us, then the fabric of all life becomes unraveled.

It therefore is an urgent question for us also as to why God hates Judah, and Jeremiah is very clear about the answer. Judah has turned totally against God in a "roaring rebellion" against him (see the lion, vs. 8). God has therefore finally turned against her and given her over into the hand of her enemy. (The verb for "lifted up" in vs. 8 is the same as that for "given" in vs. 7.) Here is that sin with a "high hand" that cannot be forgiven (Num 15:30–31), that ultimate rebellion against God's lordship that shakes its fist in his face, that sin that the church commits if it rejects its good Lord as evil and rises up against him (see Mark 3:28–30), as did some churches, for example, in Germany under Hitler's National Socialism. Let those who have ears, hear. National Socialism was destroyed, just as God's hatred and desertion of his people marked the beginning of the end of Judah.

In December of 598, Nebuchadnezzar marched against Jerusalem. In the same month, King Jehoiakim died or, more likely, was assassinated by his countrymen who hoped to gain milder treatment from Babylon. His eighteen year old son Jehoiachin (Coniah) was placed on the throne (2 Kings 24:8), but Jehoiachin's reign was short lived. After a siege of three months (see Jer 10:17–18), Jerusalem surrendered, the temple was despoiled, an enormous booty was taken, and Jehoiachin, along with his mother (see Jer 13:18–19; 22:24–30), the reigning nobles, the artisans, and the warriors were carried into Babylonian exile. Judah's territory was greatly reduced, and she was left virtually without economic means and political leadership (2 Kings 24:10–17). Jeremiah called for the professional female mourners to raise their dirge over the city (9.17–22) "Death has come up into our windows"—while the prophet himself made the reason for her fall very clear: "You have rejected me, says the LORD . . . so I have stretched out my hand against you and destroyed you" (15:6).

Prophet and Throne (21:1–23:7)

Although many of the prose sections that occur in the book of Jeremiah from chapter 25 on concern his dealings with the various kings of Judah, we have also here in this section a collection of oracles that Jeremiah delivered at various times to the occupants of the Davidic throne. Like so much else in the prophet's book, they do not stand in chronological order. 21:1–10, which is framed partly in Deuteronomic language, contains Jeremiah's reply to King Zedekiah (598–587 B.C.)

(vss. 3–7) and one of his addresses to the people of Jerusalem (vss. 8–10) in the year 588, when the city lay under Babylonian siege. 21:11–12, 13–14, and 22:1–8 are general statements of God's will for the Davidic house, dating probably from the reign of Jehoiakim (609–598 B.C.). 22:10–12 refers to the death of Josiah (626–609 B.C.) and to the deportation to Egypt of Josiah's son, Jehoahaz (Shallum), who reigned only three months in 609 B.C. 22:13–19 is an oracle directed against Jehoiakim, and 22:20–23 concerns the 597 siege of Jerusalem and the deportation of Jehoiachin (Coniah) and his mother to Babylonia. The brief oracles in 23:1–4, 5–6, 7–8 are promises for Judah's future after the Babylonian exile, but they were probably pronounced during the reign of Zedekiah.

To understand these oracles, we must first have knowledge of God's covenant with the Davidic house. In 2 Sam 7, God promises David that he will make him a house, that is, a dynasty; that there will never be lacking an heir to sit upon the Davidic throne; and that because of his promise of steadfast love to the house of David, Israel too will live in his favor forever. Such a promise was a gift of pure grace to Israel, born out of God's love for his people.

The difficulty was that Israel turned the gift into a guarantee. She felt that she could presume on God's love, that God would protect and accept her no matter what she did, that she had a Guarantor who would overlook all her rejections of him. In short, Judah believed that an eternal promise of her security had been uttered by God into history in the form of the promise to David and that therefore she could have the gift while at the same time rejecting the Giver. She did not remember that the original promise had included chastisement for sin (2 Sam 7:14), nor did she realize that God has other ways to keep his promises besides those expected by human beings. Above all, Judah did not know that the promises of God always presuppose that living relation between himself and his people, in which he is their Lord and they are his servants.

Jeremiah, however, knew that God is always Lord and that his grace cannot be claimed except in covenant love and fealty to him (see Jer 7:8–11; Rom 6:1–4). As had that Deuteronomic law, which he so urgently preached, Jeremiah therefore made Davidic king and people subject to the will of God (see Deut 17:18–20), as had every prophet before him. And like Elijah of old, Jeremiah was willing to see a throne topple rather than subvert the will of his Lord (see 1 Kings 21).

Certainly Jeremiah believed God's promise to the Davidic house. In Jeremiah's preaching, the glory of that house before God was like the lofty majesty of the mountains of Lebanon and Gilead (22:6); its authority was that bestowed on it by its Lord (22:24). Its ultimate existence was assured in God's purpose (23:5–6)—and God would be true to his promise! But as is always the case with God's promises in the OT, Jeremiah knew that between promise and eternal fulfillment must occur God's radical dealings with royal sin. That sin is nowhere more vividly portrayed than in Jeremiah's oracle concerning King Jehoiakim, in 22:13–19.

True Kingship (22:13–19). Upon the death of good King Josiah of Judah at the battle of Megiddo in 609 B.C., the people of the land put Jehoahaz, the twenty-three year old son of Josiah, on the throne (2 Kings 23:31). After three months, however, Neco II of Egypt took over parts of Syria and Palestine, summoned Jehoahaz to Riblah in central Syria, and then deported him to Egypt. In Jehoahaz' stead, Neco enthroned the twenty-five year old son of Josiah, Eliakim, changing his name to Jehoiakim (2 Kings 23:34, 36). For his part, Jehoiakim was forced to pay a heavy tribute of silver and gold, which he raised by taxing his subjects (2 Kings 23:31–35). Judah was therefore substantially impoverished at the beginning of Jehoiakim's reign. Despite this war levy and tax burden, however, Jehoiakim decided to enlarge and beautify his palace, in imitation of his Egyptian masters. In order to secure laborers for the project, he utilized the hated corvée, that is, he pressed his fellow Judeans into slave labor without wages. It is this situation that Jeremiah addresses in this oracle, probably sometime between 609–605 B.C.

In renovating his palace, Jehoiakim desired to glorify his kingship by means of greater ostentation. He added upper chambers (or an upper floor) to the building, adorned its rooms with ceilings or wainscottings of cedar painted red, and even added an "appearance window," that is, a projecting window where he could appear before the people and address them (Jer 22:14–15; see 2 Kings 9:30). But, Jeremiah asks sarcastically in vs. 15, is that what makes you a king—simply competing in cedar with other oriental despots?

In the second part of vs. 15, Jeremiah turns to the definition of true kingship, and the model that he chooses, in contrast to Jehoiakim's choice of Egyptian rulers, is the king's own father, Josiah. Josiah also lived well, says the prophet; he ate and drank; there is nothing wrong with that. But the important point is that he also did justice (*mishpat*) and righteousness (*tsedeqah*), and because he so acted, it was "well with him," that is, God showered his favor upon him, God granted him "good" (a Deuteronomic concept).

The prophet then defines what it means for a king to do justice and righteousness (vs. 16). It means to judge the cause of the poor and needy, to help them obtain their rights in the law courts and in the community proper (see 7:5–6; 22:3). The king is the guardian and guarantor of their rights, and to protect the rights of the helpless is one of the duties of kingship in Israel (see Ps 72:1–4). We can understand that, however, only if we know the meaning of "righteousness" in the OT.

"Righteousness" (*tsedeqah*) is always a relational term in the book of the Old Covenant. It signifies the fulfillment of the demands of a relationship. Here the demands of the relationship between king and subject necessitate the king's help for the poor and needy in the community. When he provides such help, he therefore is "righteous" and "just" (the terms are here synonymous).

The king has such a duty toward his subjects, moreover, because that is the way God the King also acts toward his people (see among many examples, Ps 146:7–9), and human rule is finally to be an imitation of divine rule. Therefore, when the king is righteous and just, he "knows" the Lord, that is, he knows God's character and deeds in a living relation with him, and he acts in imitation of them (Jer 22:16; see 9:23–24).

The knowledge of God is a principal theme in Jeremiah (see 2:8; 24:7; 31:34 et al.), but there is no thought here in this passage that one "knows" God by serving one's neighbor. Rather, to "know" God is to live in a relationship with him in which one knows that he is the Lord and that he delights in justice and righteousness among his people. One's actions of justice and righteousness therefore spring out of the lively fellowship with one's God. If the human king does justice and righteousness, he "knows" his Lord.

The evaluation given of Jehoiakim, then, is that he does not "know" his God; he does not do what God delights in; he does not imitate God's justice and righteousness (vs. 17). Instead, he wants and seeks nothing but his own glory and advantage, and he will do anything to obtain them. He oppresses his fellow Judeans (vs. 13); he fosters unjust judicial decisions (vs. 17); he has even murdered some, including a prophet who opposed him (vs. 17; see 26:20–23; 2:30). As is always the case in Jeremiah (see 17:1), Jehoiakim's sin is a matter of his evil heart and inner motivations, leading him to outward oppression and violence. His actions show clearly that he has no knowledge of God whatsoever, no relationship with him.

Therefore the sentence of death is pronounced on Jehoiakim (vss. 18–19), but it will be that type of death that the Hebrew feared the most—untimely, unburied, abnormal death, with no one to mourn it. When Josiah was killed, the whole country mourned (vs. 10; 2 Chron 35:24–25)—a contrast emphasized by calling Jehoiakim the son of Josiah in vs. 18—but no man or woman will shed a tear over Jehoiakim's demise. (We do not know if this prophecy was ever fulfilled. See 2 Kings 24:6.)

Obviously there are numerous points in this passage that the preacher can use in a sermon—the fact that rulers and leaders of nations are finally responsible to God (see Rom 13:1–7); that like all human beings their chief end is to glorify God and not themselves; that in the eyes of God they are "neighbors" (see vs. 13) to their subjects and must love their neighbors as themselves; but that they can never act justly and righteously toward their people except they enjoy an ongoing, continual, and vital relationship with that God who himself does justice and righteousness.

In a secular and pluralistic nation such as ours, it seems almost impossible to ensure the choice of such leaders, and to vote on the basis of such qualifications is fraught with terrible dangers. A religious leader can be a fanatic or despot, as history has often illustrated. Politicians often lay claim to a religious faith that they do not in fact possess. The Judaic-Christian faith cannot be imposed upon a pluralistic society without that imposition itself violating the most basic human rights. Nevertheless, in the exercise of our citizenship, we well might ask who a leader finally glorifies and serves and what the nature is of the God he or she professes. Is the professed deity a God of justice and righteousness, as those qualities are set forth in the Scriptures? And what is the nature of the leader's profession? Does the leader acknowledge in true humility One greater than himself or herself—greater in mercy, greater in justice, greater in understanding and power? Asking such questions surely is a part of the exercise of Christian citizenship.

The Promised King (23:5–6). This oracle, which has a somewhat altered parallel in 33:14–16 and which probably forms the original of the two pronouncements, should be read in the context of everything said above about 23:13–19. Spoken probably during the reign of King Zedekiah (598–587 B.C.), this promise for the future of a reunited Israel and Judah affirms God's covenant with David and promises that in that future God will indeed raise up a ruler from the house of David who will fulfill the demands of his relationship with God and with people. He will therefore "deal wisely" and "execute justice and righteousness in the land."

The promised ruler is called a righteous "Branch" (*tsemach*), a term used elsewhere only in Zech 3:8 and 6:12, where the reference is also to a future Davidic ruler. Isa 11:1 refers to a little "shoot" (*netser*) from the stump of Jesse—an aftergrowth, after the Davidic line has been cut off by the exile—but here the historical interruption of the Davidic line is not included.

As in Deuteronomic theology, the righteousness of this future king will serve as the righteousness of the people in the eyes of God. The life of the people is bound up in the life of its king. Therefore, they will live in God's favor. Judah will be "saved," that is, she will have room to live her life to its full,

and that is paralleled by the promise that "Israel will dwell
securely." Strife within the community itself will be gone.
Enemies will no longer threaten or destroy. Above all, God
will no longer war in wrath against his people, but will sus-
tain and guide them.

That all such future salvation is rooted in the king's living
relationship with God, however, is shown by the name he will
bear: "The Lord is our righteousness." This is a word-play on
the Hebrew term "righteousness" the main element in the
name of Zedekiah, the uncle of Jehoiachin, who was placed
on the throne in 597 B.C. by Nebuchadnezzar and who was
never considered by the Israelites to be a fully legitimate
ruler. In contrast to Zedekiah, the future ruler will truly have
his righteousness from God (see Ps 72:1), because he will live
in humble dependence on God, imitating God's actions toward his people and obeying his will. And because the king's
righteousness will be finally rooted in his continual fellowship with the Lord, so too will be the people's. Jeremiah en-
visions here a ruler and people who live and move and have
their being in their relationship with their God.

This passage and its parallel in 33:14–16 are stated OT
readings in some lectionaries for the Sunday of Christ the
King or for the first Sunday of Advent, and certainly that is a
proper use of them. No Christian can read these pericopes
without seeing their fulfillment in Jesus Christ. He is finally
the promised descendant of David (see Luke 1:32–33) who, in
perfect faith and obedience to his Lord, fulfilled all righteousness and thus made "many to be accounted righteous" (Isa
53:11). He is the promised Branch, our Ruler and our Savior.
God has kept his Word to the house of David and to his
prophet Jeremiah.

The False Prophets (23:9–40)

Apparently in Jeremiah's time the "goodly fellowship of the
prophets" was not all that goodly. Although prophets are not
listed among those against whom Jeremiah was set by God
from the beginning (1:18), Jeremiah nevertheless early in his
ministry was made aware of the corruption of the prophetic
guilds. His early oracles accuse them of prophesying by Baal
(2:8) and of worshiping Assyrian astral deities (8:1–2), of

adultery (23:13; perhaps a reference to sacred prostitution in the cult of Baal), of "wickedness" even in the temple (23:11; probably a reference to the worship of other gods), and of influencing others to follow their evil ways (23:15; 5:31). In fact, such "sons of the prophets" often directly contradicted Jeremiah's words (14:13), and a number of them were among those who wanted to kill Jeremiah because of his Temple Sermon (26:7–8, 11). Jeremiah found no moral support from other preachers, and indeed, he had to contend with their opposition throughout the course of his ministry.

Jeremiah's references to such opposition are scattered throughout his oracles, but a collection dealing with the false prophets has also been gathered together for us here in Jer 23, apparently in chronological order. 23:9–12 and 23:13–15 date probably from 621–609 B.C. 23:16–22 is an oracle dating from the reign of Jehoiakim (609–598 B.C.), 23:33–40 a prose section dating from the time of Zedekiah (597–587 B.C.).

Preachers of Success-Religion (23:16–22). The RSV has set verses 16–17 of this oracle in prose, but they too are poetry. There are additions in the lines, which the ancient Greek translation correctly omits, but that is unimportant for our purposes. Probably vss. 21–22 belong between vss. 18 and 19. Verses 19–20 are found also in 30:23–24, but they are original here.

Jeremiah's major complaint against the other prophets of his time is that they "have healed the wound of my people lightly, saying 'peace, peace,' where there is no peace" with God (6:14//8:10–12). That is, the other prophets have failed to recognize and to preach God's dissatisfaction with Judah's way of life. "You're O.K. and I'm O.K.," has been their message, and therefore "no evil will come upon you" (23:17; 5:12). Despite the fact that the Judeans despise God's Word, these false prophets tell them it will be well with them. Despite the fact that the Judeans follow only their own will and desires, the prophetic guilds assure them that they live in God's favor (23:17). "God will do nothing against you," is the message of the false prophet. "You shall see neither sword nor famine" (5:12, author's paraphrase), but rather God will give you only "assured peace" in this place (14:13).

In short, we find here in Jeremiah an early version of those preachers of success-religion, known so well in our time—preachers who believe that religion is the key to unlock the door to the good life; preachers who think that God is always kindly and forgiving and never acts against wrong; preachers who will tell people the comforting words they want to hear and never challenge their lifestyle or their actions with the Word of God's displeasure. They are the agents of the status quo, who lead their people to believe that almost anything goes in the eyes of God, who never call their people to repentance and turning from their old way of life, and who therefore actually strengthen their people in their evil ways (23:14). They cannot mediate new life to their hearers, because they find nothing wrong with the old, and so, says Jeremiah, they cannot profit and aid their people (23:32). Instead, they simply fill them with the vain hope that they are already right with God (23:16).

Such preachers and prophets obviously have not been called or sent by God (23:21, 32; 14:14). Though they claim to be speaking God's Word, they are really speaking out of their own hearts and minds (23:16, 26; 14:14). Therefore they are preaching falsely (5:31) and telling lies (23:26), perverting the Word of the living God (23:36) and sometimes just plagiarizing each other's words (23:30). It is an accusation which could be leveled against every preacher in our day who claims to preach from the Bible, but who imposes his or her own thoughts on the text or who preaches only his or her own personal opinions. Similarly, it is an accusation relevant to every preacher who, in place of meditating over and wrestling with a biblical text in exegesis and prayer, simply follows someone else's sermon outline or "borrows" someone else's sermon-thoughts.

What is the difference between such preachers and true prophets of God? In Jeremiah's language, the true prophet is one who "has stood in the council of the LORD to perceive and to hear his word," one "who has given heed to [God's] word and listened" (23:18). In the imagery of the Bible, God is enthroned in the heaven of heavens as King, surrounded by his heavenly court. In that court, decisions are made concerning life on earth (see 1 Kings 22:19–23; Job 1:6–12; Gen 1:26).

And the true prophet, says Jeremiah, is one who has been privy to that court, who has heard its decision, and who is then sent as the messenger to tell the words of the court to the inhabitants of earth.

Several of the prophetic books portray the call of the prophets in such a setting (see Isa 6:1–12; 40:1–8; perhaps the visions of Zech 1–8), and Jeremiah here claims in 23:18, 22 that from such court he has received God's words. Translated into our language, the presupposition of all true preaching, therefore, is the most intimate communion with God in prayer and study of the Scriptures, so that the true Word is written on the preacher's heart by the inspiration of the Holy Spirit. That such communion is granted only to those who exercise the continual discipline of prayer and study and meditation and action on the Word of God has been the experience of countless preachers through the ages.

The Word, then, that Jeremiah sets forth in this passage (vss. 19–20), is consistent with all his previous preaching. The whirlwind of the Lord, the storm of his wrath has gone forth, and it will not be called back, but it will burst (literally: "dance," "writhe") upon the head of the wicked in Judah. The metaphor is overwhelming: God's wrath against Judah's sin is a tornado, destroying everything in its whirling path— a frequent figure in the prophet writings (Zech 7:14; 9:14; Jer 25:32; Isa 40:24; 41:16). Over against those who have stubbornly followed the desires of their own hearts (vs. 17), there stand the intents and purposes of God's heart (vs. 20; RSV: "mind") to do away with Judah's evil. But those false prophets who have preached "peace, peace" and the good life to the Judeans have done nothing to save them from the coming storm.

God Both Near and Far (23:23–32). Most of the meaning of this prose passage has already been given in the preceding discussion, but there are three further thoughts to be added.

First, the interpreter should note the picture of God. He is not only a God at hand, that is, a little local deity, but also the majestic Holy One of Israel who—to borrow Second Isaiah's words—"sits above the circle of the earth, and its inhabitants are like grasshoppers; who stretches out the heavens like a curtain;" who calls out all the stars by name; to whom nothing and no one can be compared (Isa 40:22–26), and who fills heaven and earth, because he rules over heaven and earth (Jer 23:23).

Such an emphasis is exceedingly important for our time and in every age, for perennial popular piety tends to worship a God only near at hand—a God who comforts and guides and loves but never rules and disciplines and judges; a God so bound up with his worshipers that he never calls their actions into question; a God who has no other purpose than to give blessing to individuals. Here Jeremiah testifies to the majesty of God, who is working out an eternal purpose for his universe and who demands that human beings live their lives in accordance with that purpose. In short, Jeremiah testifies to the true nature of God. The Lord is indeed near at hand to all who call upon him in spirit and in truth. He is indeed loving and comforting and guiding. But he is also sovereign and majestic Lord above all human attempts to manipulate him. And, says the prophet, human beings delude themselves if they think to hide their deeds from such a God or to bend his will to their selfish purposes.

Second, Jeremiah discusses here the source of divine revelation, and he seems to condemn those prophets who rely on dreams (see Zech 10:2). Certainly none of the writing prophets of the OT understood the Word of God to come to them primarily through the medium of dreams. It is questionable, however, whether Jeremiah is condemning dreams as such. In earlier sources, dreams are a common medium of revelation (see Gen 20:3, 6; 31:11, 24), just as Deuteronomic writings (Num 12:6; Deut 13:1, 3; 1 Sam 28:6, 15; 1 Kings 3:5) and Joel 2:28 also assume the validity of revelations through dreams. Rather, it seems likely that the prophet is here applying the test of Deut 13:1–5 to the false prophets' dreams, since the issue at question in this passage is the nature of God and the nature of his Word. The dreams of the other prophets are false, because they corrupt the witness to God and "make my people forget my name" (vs. 27).

Third, therefore, let the dreamers tell their dreams, preached Jeremiah, and then let the people decide who speaks the true Word of God on the basis of the action of that

Word. Wheat has nothing in common with straw; wheat nourishes people, straw feeds only beasts. The Word of God does deeds, like fire consuming or like a hammer breaking rocks, but the false words of the dreamers, who speak only from their own hearts with their own tongues, are useless to do anything in the accomplishment of God's purpose. Here the prophet seems to be applying the test of Deut 18:21–22 to his opponents.

Once again the passage is relevant to modern-day preachers. Whom do they encourage the people to worship? Is he both transcendent and immanent Lord? And what do the words that they speak accomplish in the lives of their hearers?

The Burden of the Lord (23:33–40). This passage perhaps reflects the frequent inquiries made of prophets in the Judean community in the critical time of Zedekiah, when everyone, including the king, wondered what was going to happen to them before the armies of Babylonia. Apparently such inquiries had become framed most often in the question, "What is the burden of the Lord?" That is, what is the oracle or Word from the Lord concerning the situation (see Nah 1:1; Hab 1:1; Mal 1:1)? But the word for "burden" could also have the meaning of a weight or load to be carried, and in vs. 33, God replies by telling the inquirers that they are a burden to him. In other words, the Judeans should not constantly be asking for God's help when they constantly burden him with their sins (see Isa 43:22–24). Rather they should ask, "What has the Lord commanded?" or "What has the Lord required?" Then they might give heed to the true Word of God concerning their sin and their need for repentance. Because they will not listen to God's Word, however, he will cast the burden of them away from his presence—a picture of the mighty Warrior throwing the bundle of the nation into Babylonian exile. He has carried them from the womb and borne them all the ages long (see Isa 46:3–4), but now he will rid himself of their load upon him. We might well ask if we have similarly burdened and weighed down God.

Three Prose Chapters
(Jeremiah 27:1–29:32)

In 597 B.C. Nebuchadnezzar deported the Davidic Jehoiachin to Babylonia and placed on the throne of Judah in his stead his twenty-one year old uncle Zedekiah (Mattaniah), but the latter had not a ghost of a chance of bringing any stability to Judah's life (2 Kings 24:10–20). The economy of the country was crippled by Nebuchadnezzar's demands for booty, most of the leadership had been taken into exile, Judah's territory had been greatly reduced and the population cut at least in half. Worse still, Zedekiah was surrounded by an inexperienced court, some of whom favored Babylonia, but most of whom were looking for Egyptian help in revolting against their Babylonian lords. Many Judeans did not even regard Zedekiah as a legitimate king, resting their hopes instead on the exiled Jehoiachin as the only Davidic heir. At the same time, some remaining in Judah considered themselves the true remnant of God, because they had not been deported—a proud self-labeling that Jeremiah quickly contested (see Jer 24). It was a time of intrigue and of power struggles between opposing parties, and Zedekiah had neither the skill nor the authority to bring order onto the scene.

In 595, a rebellion involving officers in the Babylonian army and some among the Judean exiles broke out in Babylonia, raising the hopes of the little countries under the Babylonian yoke. The next year ambassadors from Edom, Moab, Ammon, Tyre, and Sidon met in Jerusalem to plot how to regain their freedom, perhaps encouraged also by the imminent rise of Psammetichus II (593–588 B.C.) to power in Egypt. It is these events that form the background of Jeremiah 27–28 (see 27:3).

The Contest with Hananiah (27:1–28:17)

In some versions, the superscription in 27:1 reads "Jehoiakim" rather than "Zedekiah" (see RSV margin), the name having been carried over from 26:1. The proper reading is "Zedekiah," as in the RSV.

In chapter 27, Jeremiah delivers a message to three different groups—to the foreign ambassadors (vss. 3–11), thus fulfilling his call to be "a prophet to the nations" (1:10); to Zedekiah (vss. 12–15); and to the priests and the people of Judah (vss. 16–22). To all, the message is essentially the same: do not listen to the words of the prophets and other seers (vs. 9) who are telling you that you can break free of the Babylonian yoke, for the Lord has not sent such prophets and they are telling you lies. In vss. 16–22, Jeremiah adds that the Judeans should not expect the sacred temple vessels that were carried into exile to be returned, for even the vessels still left in the temple will also be carried to Babylon. Rather, preaches the prophet, submit to the yoke of Babylonia, for if you do not, you too will be carried into exile and will die there.

Jeremiah gives one reason for such a message, and this forms the heart of the chapter: God has made the earth and all things and persons on it. He gives it to whomever he will. And he has determined that all these Near Eastern nations shall serve Nebuchadnezzar and his descendants for an appointed time (vss. 5–7; the usual figure is seventy years (see 25:12), though Nebuchadnezzar's line actually ended in 560 B.C.). Therefore, any prophet who preaches differently is not preaching the true Word of God. Moreover, as a sign of the truth of the message he is speaking, Jeremiah is commanded by God to make and to wear a wooden yoke, as symbol of Judah's subjugation to Babylonia (vs. 2).

It is an audacious claim—to say that I alone am speaking the Word of God and all the rest of you prophets are telling lies. What modern-day preacher would dare to claim as much?—although it is sobering to realize that Luther took something of the same position, just as did Karl Barth when he said "Nein" to all of eighteenth- and nineteenth-century theology.

Hananiah, the prophet from Gibeon, is quick to challenge such audacity, however, and he does so in the standard form of an oracle from the Lord (28:2). In two years, he preaches, the yoke of Babylon will be broken, the sacred vessels brought back to the temple, and King Jehoiachin (Jeconiah) returned to the throne of David (vss. 3–4). As symbol of that message, Hananiah breaks Jeremiah's wooden yoke (28:10–11).

In reply, Jeremiah expresses his own personal hope that Hananiah's words will come true (vs. 6)—a clear example of the difference between the prophet's own personal desire and the Word of the Lord—sometimes preachers have to preach words they would rather not preach! Nevertheless, Jeremiah applies Deuteronomy's test of true prophecy to Hananiah's predictions. If the word of peace comes to pass, then the prophet of peace has been sent by God (vs. 9; see Deut 18:22)—history will serve as the vindicator of the true Word of God. It is not a test that could have helped those who were trying to decide between Jeremiah's and Hananiah's positions, but in our time it highlights the importance of the church's tradition: What words from the past have stood the test of time (see 28:8)? That was one of the criteria for the formation of the canon and for the inclusion in it of the prophetic writings that we have. God did indeed fulfill these ancient words to Israel.

Despite Jeremiah's own uncertainty, God therefore tells him to replace the wooden yoke with one of iron (vs. 13)—the symbol of servitude to Nebuchadnezzar. Moreover, God's judgment on Hananiah is that he will die within the year, and in confirmation of that Word, Hananiah does indeed die (vss. 15–17)—a fact that should have convinced the wavering Judeans.

So we have here in these two chapters an interesting glimpse into the nature of true and false prophecy (see also 23:9–40). But that is not the most important message of these chapters. Rather, their central Word for us is their witness to the sovereignty of God over all nations (27:5–7; 28:14). Behind the rise and fall of empires and governments stands the Lord of history, who uses their powers as instruments of his judgment and salvation. We are not the helpless pawns of human rulers and earthly powers, but the objects of God's guidance of a sacred history. And that means that the central question of our time, as of every time, is not who is the strongest militarily, but how do we stand in the eyes of Almighty

God? In Jesus' words, "do not fear those who kill the body but cannot kill the soul; rather fear him who can destroy both soul and body in hell" (Matt 10:28)—namely, God.

For those who trust God, that is a comforting Word, for it means we are in the hands of a God whose eye is on every sparrow, who counts us infinitely more valuable than the birds of the air, who numbers the very hairs of our heads, and whose Son, if we trust him, will acknowledge us and claim us eternally as his own beloved before the Father in heaven (Matt 10:29–33).

The Letter to the Exiles (29:1–32)

Nothing came of the rebellious plans of the little Near Eastern states (27:3; see above), and indeed, Zedekiah apparently felt constrained first to send a deputation (29:3) and then personally to go to Babylon (51:59) to assure Nebuchadnezzar of Judah's continuing loyalty. Jeremiah took advantage of the deputation's trip to send a letter to the exiles in Babylon (29:4–15, 21–23; vss. 16–20 are extraneous insert).

In this letter, Jeremiah contradicts the preaching of those prophets in exile who are telling their compatriots that they will soon return to Judah (see vss. 8–9, 21–23). No, says Jeremiah, settle down for a long stay. Build houses, plant gardens, intermarry with the Babylonians, and pray for Babylon's welfare, for your life is bound up with hers for the next seventy years (vss. 5–10). At a time when Babylonia was hated and feared throughout the Near East, to a nation that had never countenanced intermarriage with foreigners (see Gen 28:1), and to Judeans who thought that God could be found only in Jerusalem (see Ps 137), that was a revolutionary message. In fact, given the political situation at the time, it was a treasonous message.

The result was that Shemaiah, a priest among the exiles, wrote the priest Zephaniah in Jerusalem, urging him to silence the "madman" Jeremiah (vss. 24–28). Perhaps in friendship, perhaps as warning, Zephaniah read the letter to the prophet, whereupon Jeremiah proclaimed that Shemaiah and his family would not live to see God's good future (vss. 29–32).

A good future, Jeremiah was sure, there would be. God had

plans for Judah. His purpose was not limited just to one generation in time any more than his sovereign working was bounded by the borders of Palestine. God had plans for Judah—good plans, to give her a future and a hope (vss. 10–11). In fulfillment of his promise in Deuteronomy (4:27–31), God would cause Judah to seek him with all her repentant and transformed heart, and so seeking, she would find him. And then God would take her back to her land (Jer 29:12–14).

In his ministry, Jeremiah now could fulfill the other half of his call (1:10). Since 626 B.C., he had preached God's words that plucked up and broke down. Now he could turn to the joyful message that God would also build and plant. God's Word of judgment is never the final Word, for God's purpose for his people is loving and good. And beyond that exile that destroyed Judah, Jeremiah was given to see God's restoration of her. That is comfort for every individual and every group that finds itself under judgment, whether that judgment take the form of "tribulation, or distress, or persecution, or famine, or nakedness, or peril, or sword" (Rom 8:35). God is finally for us, when we turn to him and seek him with all our hearts. Beyond present suffering and defeat lies his good future for us.

The Book of Comfort
(Jeremiah 30:1–31:40)

In Jer 30–31, we find a collection of miscellaneous oracles that has sometimes been called "The Little Book of Comfort." It was probably an independent collection, but then it was inserted into its present place as an introduction to the hopeful chap. 32. Certainly this collection received its present form sometime during the exilic period. Several verses in it presuppose the fall of Jerusalem (see 30:3, 8–9, 17; 31:23–26, 27–28, 38–40), and portions of the collection exhibit affinities with the preaching of Second Isaiah (see 30:10; 31:7–9, 10–14). 30:1–3 are probably an editorial superscription, while vss. 27–28, 35–37, or 38–40 of chap. 31 form the conclusion. Thus the material is not all from Jeremiah, but there are undoubtedly genuine portions. These latter include 30:5–7 and 30:12–17, both pronounced by the prophet shortly after the fall of Jerusalem. 30:23–24 has been repeated from the genuine words of 23:19–20. 31:2–6 and 31:15–22 are words that Jeremiah proclaimed to the exiled Northern Kingdom of Israel shortly after 621 B.C. 31:31–34, though often disputed by scholars, are the genuine words of the prophet, promising the new covenant. We will deal with these latter three passages in detail.

Salvation and the Ordinary Life (31:2–6)

When King Ashurbanipal of Assyria died in 627 B.C., the Assyrian empire began to totter. Josiah of Judah seized the opportunity to try to restore the kingdom of David, gradually expanding Judah's territory to reclaim the land of those ten northern tribes of Israel who had been deported in 722 B.C. In 622/1 B.C., Josiah also instituted a widespread religious reform, based on the book of Deuteronomy, in which foreign worship practices, cult sites, and clergy were purged from both north and south and all worship was centralized in Jerusalem. It was during this hopeful time that Jeremiah proclaimed this oracle to the ten northern tribes.

Verses 2–3 recall the grace that Israel first experienced

from God during her forty years of sojourn in the wilderness, after her exodus from Egypt (see Exod 33:12–17). She "sought for rest," a reference to the Deuteronomic conception of the promised land as a place of rest (see Deut 12:9; Jer 6:16; Exod 33:14). God appeared to her there (probably an allusion to Exod 33:7–11) and loved her with an everlasting love, extending to her his covenant faithfulness. That first love of God for Israel therefore foreshadowed all that would come, for now once again, the survivors of the ten northern tribes of Israel will find God's grace with them in their wilderness of Assyrian exile. From the first, God loved his helpless people, and so he shall love them always. His covenant love is the surety of all his promises for the future.

The working out of that love is emphasized by the repetitions: "Again ... Again ... Again" (vss. 4–5). The love that loved Israel at the first will not let her go. Rather, God will now fulfill his words of building and planting (Jer 1:10). Again Israel will be built—and built very securely (which is the meaning of vs. 4a). Again there will be bridal feasts (and subsequent multiplication of the population) and dancing and singing and laughing. Again there will be the normal pursuits of agriculture upon Samaria's mountains and the permanency of residence that will allow Israel to enjoy the fruits of her labor. In short, God's salvation of his exiled people will restore to them the ordinary things of life, the normal round of everyday.

Salvation, in the thought of Jeremiah, involves not some cataclysmic transformation of heaven and earth, but the restoration by God to his people of that abundant life, that good life, that he desired for them in the beginning. When God judged his people, normalcy was taken away (see 7:34; 19:9; 25:10), but in his everlasting love for his own, it will be restored. The passage is illustrative of how "this-worldly" is biblical thought and of how much value is placed on human life by the Lord. There is no escape here from history, no devaluation of human pursuits and occupations, but the affirmation that God in his love desires that there be normal life on this earth and that it be decent and good. "And God saw everything that he had made, and behold, it was very good" (Gen 1:31): that is a witness to a world-affirming God.

Moreover, formerly apostate Israel will then respond in faithfulness to God's saving love (vs. 6). Her watchers on her hills will issue the call to pilgrimage (see Ps 122:1; Jer 41:5), and her citizens will go up to Zion—the one legitimate place of worship, according to Deuteronomy. There they will worship the Lord who has saved them and confess in sincerity that he is their God.

Rachel Weeping for Her Children (31:15–20)

In Herman Melville's *Moby Dick*, Captain Ahab's search for the great white whale is interrupted one day by a plea from the captain of a passing ship, who has lost his son at sea. The latter pleads with Ahab to help find the boy and restore him to his ship, which significantly bears the name of "Rachel." Melville's use of the figure is but one illustration of the influence this moving passage from Jeremiah has had on literature. Yet, that influence is not surprising, for this poem in Jeremiah captures a perennial grief—the inconsolable weeping of a mother over her children who have somehow been lost to her. Anyone who has lost a child—to death, to indifference, to adoption, to evil influences—immediately can identify with Jeremiah's poignant portrayal of Rachel.

The text of this poem has suffered additions that mute its power. "She refuses to be comforted for her children" probably should be omitted from vs. 15. Verses 16–17 should read: "Thus says the LORD:/'Keep your voice from weeping,/and your eyes from tears,/for there is reward for your labors,/and there is hope for your future,/says the Lord.'" Verses 21–22 should not be joined to the poem. And it should be understood that God speaks throughout the poem, as if he is reporting to his prophet what he has heard.

First, God hears from the site of Ramah the voice of Rachel, the mother of the northern tribes of Ephraim, Manasseh, and Benjamin, weeping and wailing in a funeral lament, inconsolable because her children are gone. The poem does not say that the children have been taken away or that they are dead—although we know that the reference is to the Assyrian deportation of the northern tribes. Rather, the children simply "are not," which allows a universal identification with the situation. Rachel's house is left empty, and she is grief-stricken.

Ramah, which is five miles north of Jerusalem, was the site of Rachel's tomb, according to Gen 35:16–19, because she died in childbirth on the way from Bethel to Ephrath. In Gen 35:19 and 48:7, Ephrath is confused with Ephrathah, another name for Bethlehem (see Ruth 4:11; Mic 5:2), which was south of Jerusalem, and this confusion has passed into the NT (Matt 2:18). It is not to be thought that Jeremiah is portraying here Rachel speaking from the dead. Rather, the prophet is using poetic metaphor. Rachel, the symbolic mother of the northern tribes, weeps, and God hears her weeping.

God therefore tells the grief-stricken mother to cease from lamentation, because there will be a reward for her labors and hope for her future, through her children (vss. 16–17). All her motherly care and concern and work for her offspring will not have been in vain, but will bear fruit and issue in a good and fine life for her family. The life of Rachel's children has been brought to a standstill, but God assures her that is not the end. Her children will yet fully live, and there is yet therefore hope for the future.

In vs. 18, God then goes on to explain to Rachel why this is so. He has heard Ephraim, the child of Rachel, bemoaning his own sin. God's destruction of the Northern Kingdom has been the discipline the heavenly Father has given his son, and Ephraim now realizes this. He has accepted God's disciplining of him, because he now realizes that he was formerly uncontrolled, like some calf untrained to the yoke (see Jer 2:20; Hos 4:16; 10:11). But then, he came to himself, and repented, and smote himself upon the thigh, an expression of grief and shame over the sins he had committed against God (vs. 19). And so he prays that God will let him return to fellowship with him, in the covenant relationship (vs. 18). He does not ask for return from exile, but simply for restoration of his relationship with God. That now is the one important goal in repentant Ephraim's eyes.

In vs. 20, God therefore replies to Ephraim's repentant prayer and affirms that Ephraim is still his son. It is not only Rachel who grieves over Ephraim; God also grieves over him.

And so every time God speaks in judgment against Ephraim, he remembers that he is his son. And he yearns for Ephraim's return to him, with a depth of longing possible only to God. He therefore will have mercy on his son and let him return and restore him to his family.

As has often been remarked, we have here the OT equivalent of the story of the prodigal son (Luke 15:11-32). The basic reason that there is hope for Rachel's future—and this is all vision of the future in Jeremiah—is because Rachel's children are God's children. We dare to say that even apart from Ephraim's repentance, God loves him to the depth of his divine being, and he therefore will have mercy on him. That is hope that transcends all weeping and despair.

In interpreting this passage from the pulpit, there are various levels of meaning that could be drawn from it. First and foremost, of course, the passage has to do with our relationship with God, just as does the parable of the prodigal son. And in that relationship, this passage emphasizes the importance of our repentance. But perhaps there is also a message here for all of those sorrowing parents who have lost their children to whatever evil in the world and who despair of ever having a relationship with them again. Such children too are God's children, and God shares the grief of their parents. His mercy will follow such errant children to the ends of the earth and beyond. And because our children are finally in God's good hands, there is eternal hope.

The New Covenant (31:31-34)

Some have held that this famous passage in Jeremiah also was originally directed to northern Israel in the hopeful time of Josiah, shortly after 621 B.C. and that it was then expanded in vs. 31 to include Judah, after the exile of that nation in 587 B.C. I am more inclined to date it as a whole about 586 B.C., during the time of Gedaliah. But certainly it should be treated by the preacher as it now stands, and no pericope from Jeremiah's message is more important.

We find here God's solution to the sin of his people. In the early preaching of his prophet, God held out the invitation to his sinful people to mend their ways and to return to him. But they would not. To every gracious invitation from God, they replied, "That is in vain! We will follow our own plans, and will every one act according to the stubbornness of his evil heart" (Jer 18:12). In fact, they not only rejected God's grace, but also mocked his Word, spoken through Jeremiah, and they persecuted the prophet. Their sin had such a grip on them that they no longer had any power of self-assessment (see Jer 8:4–7), and they had become unable by their own power to repent. "Can the Ethiopian change his skin or the leopard his spots?" God asked. "Then also you can do good who are accustomed to do evil" (Jer 13:23). As in the letters of Paul, they were slaves to sin (Rom 6:17, 20, 22), or as in Hosea, their deeds did not permit them to return to God, for the spirit of harlotry was in them and they knew not the Lord (Hos 5:4). Their sin, rather than God's Word, was written with a point of diamond on their hearts (17:1), and unless somehow their hearts were changed, there was no hope for them.

Such history of Israel's and Judah's sin is summed up in vss. 31 and 32 of this passage. Despite God's grace—despite the fact that he took his people by the hand and led them, like a father his son, out of captivity in Egypt and made a covenant with them at Sinai, and then renewed that covenant with them in the Deuteronomic reform—despite the whole long history of God's mercy toward his covenant people—they nevertheless broke covenant faithfulness with him. He was their husband—to change the figure to the one here used— the one who had so tenderly loved them in the wilderness (see 2:2). Yet, Israel whored after other lovers (see 2:23–25), and gave her devotion to other gods and goddesses (see Jer 7:17–18, 30–31). God therefore rejected them as his people and sent them into exile (see 12:7).

But God never gives up on his chosen folk. He never delivers them forever into the hands of their enemies or into captivity and evil and death. At the same time, he never softens or lays aside his demand for faithfulness from his people. He cannot simply overlook their sinful hearts and accept them, faithless and rebellious as they are, for in his love, God knows that fealty to him is the only way to abundant life. And he will have nothing less for his people than that good life, pressed down and running over.

God therefore adopts the one solution for sin that is possible. He will in the future, says this passage, change his people's sinful hearts (see Jer 32:39–40; Ezek 36:26–27). He will transform them from the inside out, so that in place of the sin written upon their hearts there will be his law, and therefore the people will be able to obey him, in faithfulness and in love (see Deut 6:4–6). Their sinful past will be forgotten—God will forgive it all—and they will be reunited with him in a new covenant relationship of devotion and gratitude and obedience. Indeed, so thorough will be God's transformation of the hearts of his people that no one will have to teach his or her neighbor about the character of God. All will know him, in an intimate relationship like that of a faithful wife with her husband. All will cleave to him and follow him and love him with all their hearts. What his people could not do for themselves, God will do for them in an act of pure mercy and love. Such is the hopeful future that Jeremiah is given to see for his exiled people.

It is obvious from this passage why moralistic preaching does no good. It does not and it cannot produce any change in people's lives, for they have no power in themselves to change. Exhortations to repent, to obey God, to live new lives in accordance with his will are powerless to enable sinners to repent and to return to the Lord. They are prisoners—slaves of sin—and exhorting prisoners to be good is like telling them to fix up their prison cages a little—maybe to hang a picture on the wall or to put a rug on the floor. But what is needed is someone to come and open the door! What is needed is a Savior who will free them from their captivity to sin. And that is what God promises his erring people in this new covenant—freedom from their imprisonment, freedom from their slavery to sin, and power given them to do the right and to live new lives of faithfulness to their Lord.

This was a promise made by God for Judah's future. The question therefore is, Did God keep his promise? That question should always be asked of the OT. What happened to its ancient words? Were they fulfilled? Did they come to pass? Or were they allowed to fall by the way and disappear into the sands of time?

The testimony of the NT, then, is that God kept this ancient promise to his covenant folk. "The Lord Jesus on the night when he was betrayed took bread. . . . In the same way also the cup, after supper, saying, 'This cup is the new covenant in my blood'" (1 Cor 11:23–25; see Matt 26:28; Mark 14:24; Luke 22:20). God replaced his old covenant, which his people broke, with his new covenant in Jesus Christ and thereby made it possible for his covenant people to live new lives of faithfulness and obedience (see Heb 8:8–12; 10:16–17).

Moreover, says Paul, God has written this new covenant upon our hearts by the work of the Holy Spirit. His love has been poured into our hearts through the Holy Spirit (Rom 5:5). He has sent the Spirit of his Son into our hearts, so that we are no longer slaves but heirs (Gal 4:6–7). He "has shone in our hearts to give the light of the knowledge of the glory of God in the face of Christ" (2 Cor 4:6). Christians therefore no longer serve under an old written code, but in the new life of the Spirit (Rom 7:6). Though we were once slaves of sin, we now can be obedient from the heart to the will of God (Rom 6:17). In short, Christians now have the possibility not to sin (Augustine: *posse non peccare*)—not by their own power, but solely by the power of God working in them. Paul's admonition to us is, "Let not sin therefore reign in your mortal bodies" (Rom 6:12). In the power of Jesus Christ, lent to us by the Spirit, we can in truth become new creatures and lead a new life of faithfulness.

Like so much of the OT message that finds its fulfillment in the NT, however, this promise of the new covenant in Jeremiah has not yet fully been fulfilled. The fulfillment is "already," but also "not yet." We have been made new creatures in Jesus Christ, but our perfect obedience awaits that time when the Spirit, given us as a guarantee, will have wholly changed us into the image of Christ (2 Cor 3:18) and we are presented before the Father "without spot or wrinkle or any such thing . . . holy and without blemish" (Eph 5:27).

Further, this promise of the new covenant in Jeremiah has not yet fully been fulfilled, because all people do not yet know the Lord, from the least of them to the greatest, and all people have not yet, in faith, received the Spirit of Christ into their hearts. And so we are given the ministry of evangelism, of spreading the good news that new life is possible in Jesus Christ. Once again, in Paul's words, "Not that we are [sufficient] of ourselves . . . our [sufficiency] is from God, who has [qualified] us to be ministers of a new covenant, not in a written code but in the Spirit; for the written code kills, but the Spirit gives life" (2 Cor 3:5–6). All Christians are sent into all the world, not only to live but also to proclaim that new life in the Spirit.

Jerusalem Under Siege
(Jeremiah 21; 32; 34–35; 37–38)

The Purchase of Hope (chap. 32 [21 and 27])

According to the superscription of chap. 32 (vss. 1–2), its events take place in 588 B.C. during the time that Jerusalem is under siege by the Babylonians and Jeremiah is a prisoner in the court of the palace guard. We cannot understand this chapter unless we sketch the events that have led up to such a situation.

In 593 B.C., Psammetichus II assumed the throne of Egypt, and both he and his son Hophra (Apries; 588–569 B.C.) resumed the policy of interfering in the affairs of Asia and Palestine. Such a resurgence of Egyptian power fanned the fires of rebellion that had smouldered in Judah since 597, and by 589 B.C. that country, along with Tyre and Ammon, was in open revolt against its Babylonian masters. Nebuchadnezzar, however, was completely in control. He established his headquarters at Riblah in Syria, and in January of 588 B.C., his troops placed Jerusalem under blockade. His strategy was very simple, as can be seen in Jer 34:7. He simply took, one by one, the outlying fortifications surrounding Jerusalem, until finally only the fortresses of Lachish and Azekah were left. In fact, in a letter discovered at the site of ancient Lachish, the officer in charge of an outpost writes to the garrison commander at Lachish that he can no longer see Azekah's signal fires. Having destroyed her outlying fortifications by the summer of 588 B.C., Nebuchadnezzar's troops then lay siege to the city itself.

In the middle of that desperate military situation, Jeremiah played the traitor. As can be read in chap. 21, he preached to both king and people, "He who stays in this city shall die by the sword, by famine, and by pestilence, but he who goes out and surrenders to the Chaldeans (Babylonians) who are besieging you shall live and shall have his life as a prize of war" (vs. 9). Jeremiah was convinced by the Word of God that not just the Babylonians were fighting against them, but the Lord himself, and that the only way Zedekiah and Judah could live was to surrender to Babylonia. In the light of such apparent treason, it is amazing that the Judeans did not arrest Jeremiah on the spot, but apparently some nobles in the city also thought the case was hopeless, because the Lachish letters also complain that nobles "weaken the hands" of the people.

In a panic of desperation-religion, Zedekiah and the Judeans decided that perhaps their hope lay in obedience to God's will after all, as it was set forth in the Deuteronomic law. They therefore held a covenant renewal ceremony, and as a sign of their good faith, they proclaimed the year of release for Hebrew slaves, according to the command of Deut 15:1, 12–18 (Jer 34:8–10; compare vs. 16 with Deut 21:14). As if in answer to such "foxhole religion," news arrived of an approaching Egyptian force, and the Babylonians were forced to lift the siege, whereupon the Judeans immediately forgot about covenant obedience and took back their slaves (Jer 34:11–16). God's reaction through his prophet was fierce: the Babylonians would return, he said—which they soon did— the city would be burned with fire and Judah made a desolation (Jer 34:17–22; 37:3–10).

During the lifting of the siege, Jeremiah tried to leave Jerusalem to redeem a piece of family property that had fallen to him by right of inheritance (37:11–21). At the gate of the city, he was arrested by a sentry, charged with deserting to the Babylonians, and taken before the city leaders. Enraged, they beat him and threw him into a dungeon cell, where he probably would have died if it had not been for King Zedekiah, who sent for him secretly to inquire of him a Word from the Lord. In the secret conversation, Jeremiah had no hope to offer the fearful Zedekiah, but he did convince him to transfer him from the dungeon prison to the court of the palace guard. There, Jeremiah at least had food, he had a certain measure of freedom to walk about in the courtyard, and he could and did continue to shout out to passersby to surrender to Nebuchadnezzar's troops (see 38:2–4).

The picture of Jerusalem under Babylonian siege shows the most appalling conditions. Food and water rations were severely taxed, and Jeremiah (19:9), Ezekiel (5:10), and the book of Lamentations (2:12, 19–20; 4:4, 7–10) all tell us that toward the end of the siege, parents were driven to eating the flesh of their children. Epidemics and disease swept through the weakened and crowded population. Material property, of course, was of absolutely no value. Silver and gold were worthless, because there was nothing to buy. All commercial enterprises collapsed, because there was nothing to sell. Property values plummeted, as they always do in war, because everyone was trying to sell property and to flee the city. Who wanted any land when the Babylonians were knocking at the gates?

It is in this situation that the Word of the Lord came to Jeremiah. "Buy my field which is at Anathoth in the land of Benjamin, for the right of possession and redemption is yours; buy it for yourself" (32:8). And I knew, says the prophet to us, that this was the Word of the Lord.

Jeremiah had earlier tried to buy that land, as we saw in 37:11–15, had been beaten up and arrested, and had given up the enterprise as not worth the trouble. Besides, it had seemed like a very unprofitable purchase in the light of Judah's situation. But now the prophet hears that God has a hand in the enterprise. God wants him to buy the land. How hidden are the ways of God sometimes in this secular world! And as might be expected, the command is totally incomprehensible to Jeremiah. "Behold, the siege mounds have come up to the city to take it," he prays, "Yet thou, O Lord God, hast said to me, 'Buy the field . . .'" (32:24–25). Now, when everything looks hopeless. When fields and farms are not worth a penny. When there seems to be no hope, because the world is crumbling about us, and the only thing worth doing seems to be to survive by any means here and now, and never mind the consequences. When our terrible, weak, blind, human failures have got us into this mess, and we can no longer stand to analyze the guilty past or to look forward to the awful future that we have determined for ourselves. When we try to shut out memory, shut out hope, and just try to stay alive.

But the Word is not, "Guard what you have, Jeremiah. Hide your scraps of bread and your cup of water from those who peer hungrily into your courtyard. Never mind what's happening outside in the street. Look out for yourself." No, the

Word is, "Buy a field." And the reason for that command to the prophet is given in vs. 15: "For thus says the LORD of hosts, the God of Israel: Houses and fields and vineyards shall again be bought in this land."

That is the Word of the Lord that comes to us from this passage in Jeremiah—that when everything is hopeless on our human scene, God still has a plan for the future. When we stand beside the grave of a loved one, and all the pain floods over us; when we realize that we can never more say what we wanted to say and can never more do what we wanted to do for that dead one—God has a plan. When everything lovely and gracious and pure in our world seems to fall victim to corruption and evil; when no good work seems to endure and no project of love seems to bear lasting fruit; when every act we do is tainted by selfishness—God has a plan. When the meek, the peacemakers, the pure in heart, get trampled into the dirt; when the weak constantly are sacrificed on the altars of power and the tongues of the proud and mighty strut through the earth –God has a plan. When there seems to lie ahead of us nothing but a crucifixion; when the Gethsemane of prayer is darkened by the shadow of a looming Golgotha; when we would rather do any other thing than obey the will of the Father and we cry out to him to remove this cup from us—God has a plan.

It is a plan of love to save us and our world, despite the fact that we, like Judah, deserve nothing but God's condemnation of death. It is a plan to re-create the good and abundant and eternal life on earth that God intended for his world in the beginning. It is a plan to make a new people, a new community, that knows how to live together in justice and peace and righteousness, under the lordship of God. And so, in chap. 32, we see God patiently, step by step, working out that plan for the future (see Deut 30:1–8).

First, in vs. 37, God promises to restore the communal life of the people of God. Then he says he will renew the covenant relationship that Judah has so wantonly broken (vs. 38), transforming the hearts of his people so that they will live obedient lives (vss. 39–40). Finally, God promises to do good to his people, never to turn away from them, and he promises that with all his divine heart and soul (vs. 41). Were ever more merciful words pronounced? God will do good to his people, with all his heart and soul! Surely that is the promise he has kept for us in our Lord Jesus Christ (see on Jer 31:31–34)!

Covenant Renewed and Broken (34:1–35:19)

We have already illumined the events in chap. 34 in the preceding discussion of chap. 32. One further point should be emphasized: the readiness of God to forgive and to save his sinful people. When the people surrender themselves to God's will and obey the law of Deuteronomy (15:1, 12–18), they are "right" in his eyes (Jer 34:15), and the implication of the passage is that God will deliver them from the judgment he has determined against them. Despite all their sin, despite the years of apostasy and rebellion and lack of knowledge of their Lord, documented in the preaching of Jeremiah, God will look with favor on his people when they turn and do his will. How very ready is this God to forgive, to build, and to plant!

We must not think that we have here in Jeremiah some sort of legalism, however—that righteousness in the eyes of God comes by works of the law. No, at the heart of the Deuteronomic law is the command to love God with all one's heart and mind and strength (Deut 6:5), to give him one's trust, to cleave to him, as an obedient son to his father. The requirement of God in Deuteronomy, as in the preaching of Jeremiah, is for whole-hearted surrender to the love and will of one's Lord. And the fact that such surrender is involved in this passage of Jer 34 is shown by the play on the word "liberty" (vss. 8, 15, 17). The command of God in Deuteronomy is that the Hebrew, in obedience and love for God, give liberty to his slave. But when the Judeans turn that around—when they proclaim liberty from God and deny liberty to their slaves—then God will indeed proclaim liberty to them—"to the sword, to pestilence, and to famine" (vs. 17). Liberty from God—unbridled freedom (see Jer 2:20–32), following one's own will and desire—lead not to life but to death (see Gen 3). And God's judgment is that rebellious humankind can have the liberty to die that it has chosen (see Rom 1:26–32).

As illustration, chap. 35, concerning the faithfulness of the Rechabites to their vow to God, follows immediately on chap. 34. In obedience to God's command (see Num 6:2–4; Judg

13:7, 14; Lev 10:9; Luke 1:15), they had covenanted to drink no wine or live the urban life of Canaan—a protest against the baalization of Hebrew life—and their faithfulness is contrasted with the faithlessness of rebellious Judah. The Rechabites will therefore be rewarded for their faithfulness (vs. 19), while Judah will be destroyed (vss. 15–17). The way of life consists in cleaving, with all one's heart and in all one's deeds, to our sovereign Lord.

Blindness, Mercy, and Cheap Grace (38:1–28)

There are some scholars who hold that this chapter is another version of the events in chap. 37, but it is more likely that it recounts the final threat to Jeremiah's life. From his prison in the court of the guard (37:21), the prophet continued to call out to passersby to surrender to the Babylonians and save their lives, for Jerusalem would surely be taken (38:2–3). Some of the Judean nobles therefore demanded of the vacillating King Zedekiah that Jeremiah be put to death for his treason, and Zedekiah had no power to oppose them. The princes lowered Jeremiah into a muddy cistern in the court of the guard and left him to starve to death in that miry grave (vs. 6). Saved by the humanitarianism of a court eunuch and by a suddenly repentant Zedekiah (vss. 7–13), Jeremiah was once more asked for a Word from the Lord by the king (vss. 14–16). But his message to the ruler was the same: if the city would surrender to the Babylonians, it would not be destroyed and Zedekiah would not be killed (vss. 17–18). When the king voiced his fear that if he surrendered he would be abused by the Jews who had already deserted to the enemy, the prophet assured him that such would not be the case (vss. 19–20). But that was the only reassurance Jeremiah could give the king. He did, however, lie to the princes in order to protect the king against them (vss. 24–28).

Perhaps most noteworthy in this chapter are the character studies presented to us. First, there are the princes—secular men, who know nothing about the Word and will of God but only about the ways of the world. They have power over their human king, but they do not understand that God the King has power over them. Thus, they can orchestrate events only on the basis of their limited human wisdom, and it is clear to them that Jeremiah "is not seeking the welfare of this people, but their harm" (vs. 4). Jeremiah's God is trying to save their lives and city, but because they "are wise in their own eyes, and shrewd in their own sight," they "call evil good and good evil" (Isa 5:20–21) in a blind refusal of mercy. Such secular blindness can never see the world as it really is, for it shuts its eyes to the real power in the world, namely God.

Second, there is the Ethiopian eunuch Ebed-melech, whose name, in a prophetic word-play, means "servant of the (divine?) king." He is a man undoubtedly captured during a battle and then enslaved to serve the royal household, but also castrated to prevent the use of any sexual prowess among the women of the court. He is not a worshiper of the God of Israel, and he does not plead for Jeremiah on the basis of religious morality. Rather, he is simply a humanitarian, who does not like to see a fellow human being die (vs. 9). When he lifts Jeremiah from the cistern, he shows the greatest tenderness by padding the ropes (vs. 12)—something the princes had not done, of course (vs. 6)—and when Jerusalem falls, he is rewarded for his kindness by the Lord (39:15–17; see the reward of Baruch's service to the prophet, chap. 45). Thus do sometimes the merciful acts of pagans put to shame the far less merciful deeds of supposedly religious practitioners. (See Luke 10:29–37; note also the church's failure to take the initiative in the civil rights and women's movement.)

Third, we have portrayed here and in the preceding chapters the fearful and almost pitiable King Zedekiah. His circumstances are such that it is almost impossible for him to rule. His country is impoverished and besieged; pro-Egyptian and nationalist parties oppose him; many do not even consider him their legitimate king. But the pertinent facts about Zedekiah have to do with his relation to God. There is no indication that Zedekiah has any loyalty to the Lord, despite his name which means "the Lord is my righteousness."

Jeremiah asks two conditions of Zedekiah in this chapter: one, that he not put him to death, and two, that he listen to his counsel (vs. 15). Zedekiah promises to honor only the first condition (vs. 16), because Zedekiah is a man who never hears what he likes from the Lord (see 1 Kings 22:8). Repeatedly he sends for the prophet to ask from him a Word from God (21:2)

or to bid Jeremiah to pray for deliverance (37:3). "Perhaps the
LORD will deal with us according to all his wonderful deeds,"
says Zedekiah, "and will make [Nebuchadnezzar] withdraw
from us" (21:2). Zedekiah wants cheap grace from God, with
nothing required in return—no repentance, no amendment
of life, no heartfelt trust, no faithful obedience—a new life
without the death of the old, a resurrection without a crucifixion. To an age such as ours, that so often wants the same
easy grace, it is instructive to ponder Zedekiah's end (see
below).

The Fall of Jerusalem and Afterward
(Jeremiah 39:1–44:30)

Judgment Accomplished (39:1–10)

God kept the words that he pronounced through his prophet Jeremiah. God always keeps his Word. In July of 587 B.C., the walls of Jerusalem were breached by the Babylonians and the populace surrendered, the princes of Babylonia holding trials of various Judeans in the middle gate of the city (39:1–3; a fulfillment of 1:15–16). King Zedekiah and some of his troops attempted to escape by night toward the Jordan Valley, but they were captured near Jericho and taken to Nebuchadnezzar at Riblah, where he passed sentence upon them. Zedekiah's sons were slain before his eyes. He was then blinded and taken in chains to Babylon, where he died in prison. At the same time, the temple was denuded of its valuable furnishings and then put to the torch, along with the rest of the city. The walls of Jerusalem were reduced to rubble, and some 832 men and their familes were carried into Babylonian exile, to join those already deported in 597 B.C. (Jer 52:1–30; 39:4–10). Judah was now ended as a nation, in fulfillment of the Word of the Lord.

We in our time, with our comfortable views of God, do not think that he would bring such judgment upon his chosen people. Consequently, we reduce this story of destruction and others like it in the OT to the status of purely secular events, with which God has absolutely nothing to do. The fall of Jerusalem, we like to maintain, was simply a historical happening, brought about by the clash of human empires.

Of course that was also the view of the populace of Judah in Jeremiah's time. They never believed the prophet when he told them that God would wipe out their sin by destroying them as a nation. They never acknowledged their own sinfulness, much less the displeasure of God with them, and so they did not repent in time. Indeed, their sin became so ingrained in their hearts that they could not repent.

We similar secularists, however, have been offered release from our sin and its accompanying death by God's merciful act in the crucifixion and resurrection of Jesus Christ. And so when the final judgment comes, our Lord's question to us is, "When the Son of man comes, will he find faith on the earth?" (Luke 18:8).

Jeremiah Remains with His People
(39:11–14//40:1–6)

Apparently those Babylonian princes responsible for deciding the cases of the inhabitants of Jerusalem (39:3) brought Jeremiah from his prison in the court of the guard (39:14) and, on orders from Nebuchadnezzar (39:11–13), gave him the choice of traveling freely to Babylon or of remaining in devastated Judah under the governorship of Gedaliah (40:2–6; vs. 1 is perhaps nongenuine; the order of the text in 39:11–14 is disturbed; the Greek version omits 39:4–13). Jeremiah chose to remain with Gedaliah, a member of one of the reform families with whom Jeremiah had long been associated (see the section on Jeremiah and the Deuteronomic Reform).

But was Jeremiah's choice made simply on the grounds of his love for his country, his association with the reformers, and his sympathy with his suffering people? That all seems doubtful. If we are correct in dating Jeremiah's proclamation of the new covenant (31:31–34) from this period, the prophet remained in his devastated land to proclaim God's future to Judah. In the midst of ruin, God promised restoration; in the midst of death, coming life. God's work of plucking up and breaking down was now complete; building and planting were to follow (see 1:10). And so it has always been with the Word of God (see Jer 32). At the very extremity of life, when all seems done and the future nonexistent, the Word sounds forth that the Lord is not finished with his people. He is never finished, until his kingdom comes on earth, even as it is in heaven.

Gedaliah, Ishmael, and the Flight to Egypt
(40:7–16; 41:1–18; 42:1–43:13)

The new governor, Gedaliah, shared Jeremiah's faith. He knew that in God's purpose, there was a future for his country. He therefore began the work of reconstruction, urging upon his people submission to their Babylonian rulers and industry in agriculture and restoration (40:7–12). Knowing that the future was in God's hands, he bent to the tasks assigned to him without worry, without fear, without despair. He was a perfect symbol of a man of faith who was not "anxious about tomorrow" (see Matt 6:25–33). But he was also a little naïve. When he was warned of the plot against his life, he did not believe it (40:13–16). He was harmless as a dove, but not as wise as a serpent (Matt 10:16). We can, it seems, from our Lord's teaching, trust the goodness of God to provide for our lives, without closing our eyes to the evil in the hearts of human beings.

The result was that Gedaliah and his government officials, along with a number of Babylonian soldiers, were assassinated by a group, under the leadership of Ishmael ben Nethaniah, that opposed the policy of collaboration (41:1–3). Wreaking havoc as they went, the assassins then fled toward Ammon, taking with them the remaining Jews at Mizpah, including Jeremiah (41:4–10). The hostages were quickly freed by a pursuing posse under the leadership of Johanan ben Kareah, but Ishmael and eight of his men escaped (41:11–15).

The question then however was, How would Babylonia react to the murder of Gedaliah and of some of its soldiers? To be sure, Johanan and his company had had nothing to do with the assassination, but would Babylonia not bring retribution on the whole of Judah's remnant for the hotheaded actions of a few (41:16–18)? Should that remnant not therefore flee to Egypt to prevent their being exiled also? The fearful group decided to ask Jeremiah to pray to the Lord for guidance in the critical situation, and they promised, with an oath, that they would do whatever the Lord told them through his prophet to do (41:1–6).

For ten days, the Lord gave Jeremiah no reply—an indication of the prophet's total dependence on God and not on his own wisdom, but perhaps also a test of the impatient remnant's faith (42:7). When the answer did come, it was full of mercy. God was with the Judeans; he would influence Nebuchadnezzar to allow them to remain in Judah; there God would "build" and "plant" his remaining people and do "good" to them, that is "save" them (42:8–12, see vs. 6).

The remnant of Judah was being asked to place their faith

in God's unknown future. They had escaped with their lives
from days of siege and ruin, in which they had seen the destruction of battle and heard the terrifying sound of the war
trumpet and felt hunger's pangs gnawing at their stomachs
(vs. 14). According to Jeremiah, God had brought all that
upon them. Now they were being asked to trust the same God
to deliver them from such terrors and to give them once again
a good and peaceful life. They were being asked to believe
that the same God who plucked up and broke down was in
the future going to build and to plant.

The decision facing this desperate little band was the decision that always confronts persons of faith. Do we believe
that in good times and bad God wills only good for us? Do we
trust that the suffering and troubles that come upon us may
be as much a part of God's loving will for us as the peace and
prosperity we know? Could the Judeans believe that God's
destruction of their land was an act finally taken for their
salvation? Could our Lord believe that the cross that loomed
before him was included in God's good purpose? And so could
the Judeans, and Jesus, and can we believe, no matter what
sufferings we go through, that God is at work to lead us mer-
cifully into his abundant life for us? And therefore will we
trust our future to his hands and obey his guidance of us?

Unless a faith is present that has learned to place all things
in the hands of God, we cannot—and the Judeans did not—
answer yes to any of those questions. Johanan and his company opted for Egypt. Once more, following their pattern of
years, they turned their back on Jeremiah's words from God.
And so they chose death instead of life, for "he who would
save his life shall lose it."

Worst of all, Johanan and his band forced Jeremiah and his
scribe Baruch to accompany them to Egypt, where they
settled at Tahpanhes (Daphne), in northeastern Egypt (43:1–
7; see 2:16). But if they thought to escape the hand of Babylonia, Jeremiah preached to them otherwise. In a symbolic
action (43:8–13), he announced that Nebuchadnezzar would
come into Egypt and execute God's promised judgments on
those unfaithful to him. We know that Nebuchadnezzar did
in fact invade Egypt in 568/7 B.C., in a punitive raid, but we
have no further knowledge of Johanan and his followers.

Jeremiah's Final Preaching (44:1–30)

The last glimpse we have of the prophet is of him still faithfully fulfilling his mission, preaching the Word of the Lord to all those Jews in Egypt, who had fled their devastated country in Palestine and scattered throughout the regions around the mouth of the Nile. Ironically, Jeremiah's preaching had to deal with the same subject he had dealt with in the early days of his ministry—with the apostasy of his compatriots, who were worshiping pagan gods and goddesses, specifically "the Queen of Heaven," who is probably here to be identified with the Assyrian-Babylonian goddess Ishtar.

The prophet pointed out to these Jews that they were committing the same sins that had brought God's judgment on Judah and Jerusalem in the form of Babylonia (vss. 2–6, 20–23), and that the continuance of such apostasy would bring judgment on the remnant in Egypt also, leaving them with no heirs to return to Palestine, other than a few fugitives (vss. 11–14, see vss. 27–28).

But the answer that the Jews gave to the prophet at an assembly (called for the purpose?) was a direct contradiction of Jeremiah's interpretation of their past (44:15–19). God was not working for their welfare, the Jews said. Rather, their best hope lay with Ishtar, for when they had burned incense and poured out libations to her, they had had plenty of food and prospered—probably a reference to the relatively undisturbed time of 626–609 B.C., when no foreign power dominated their life and when idolatrous worship practices continued, despite the reform measures of 622/1 (see Jer 7:16–20). It was only when, in obedience to the Deuteronomic reform or to the prophet's word, they ceased worshiping the Queen of Heaven that their situation took a turn for the worse. The God of Israel was not in charge of their fate; Ishtar was; therefore they vowed that they would worship her (vss. 18–19, 24–25).

The Judeans made two fatal errors. First, they chose their deities on the basis of their material welfare. The only divinities they desired were those who promised them "peace, peace" and comfort. Had such been the attitude of all the people of God, there would today be no biblical faith. And

had such been the attitude of our Lord in the garden of Gethsemane, there would be no Christian church.

Second, the Judeans interpreted what happened to them
on the basis of their own sagacity, rather than on the basis of
the Word of God. But human history is opaque. It never gives
a clear witness to who is in charge of the world's events. Read
on the basis of human wisdom, often no one seems in charge.
Only when the interpreting Word is spoken by God's prophets
or apostles or, in these latter days, by his Son (see Heb 1:1),
are the myriad happenings of human life seen in their proper
context of God's will and given their true meaning by the
light of God's sovereign purpose. We do not know where the
world is going or what we should do or what will become of
us except we know what God says in his Word. Only in that
Word is human life given sense and direction.

To that Word alone Jeremiah points at the end of his
preaching. "All the remnant of Judah, who came to the land
of Egypt to live, shall know whose Word will stand, mine or
theirs," he proclaims in the name of the Lord (vs. 28). Moreover, to prove that God's Word alone will stand, a sign is
added to it: Pharaoh Hophra (Apries) will be assassinated by
his enemies (vss. 29–30), a prophecy evidently fulfilled in a
rebellion against Hophra in 570 B.C.

Some say that vss. 29–30 were added to the book of Jeremiah after 570. However that may be, they are unimportant
for us, for we do not need their particular sign. We need only
ask, Whose Word has stood through the ages? Whose Word of
judgment has been confirmed in the history of his chosen
people, and whose Word of mercy has been found by countless faithful souls never to fail or to forsake them? God has
proved true. He has kept his Word in the history of Israel, in
the history of the Christian church, and above all, in Jesus
Christ. And so we know that though heaven and earth should
pass away, God's Word will not pass away. It stands. It shall
ever stand. Let us therefore keep that Word and walk by it,
and find therein our hope and our salvation.

The Conclusion of the Collection
(Jeremiah 46:1–52:34)

Oracles Against the Foreign Nations (46:1–51:64)

The final prophetic oracles found in the book of Jeremiah are a miscellaneous collection announcing God's judgment on Israel's enemies: Egypt (46:1–26); Philistia (47:1–7); Moab (48:1–47); Ammon (49:1–6); Edom (49:7–22); Damascus (49:23–27); various Arab tribes (49:28–33); Elam (49:34–39); and Babylonia (50; 1–3, 8–16, 21–27, 29–32, 35–46; 51:1–14, 20–44, 47–58). These are interspersed with various poems announcing the restoration of Israel to her land, and with prose comments. 46:1 serves as the superscription to the collection, and the final sentence of 51:64 was probably its conclusion, while 51:59–64 is the account of a prophetic symbolic action. In the ancient Greek version, chaps. 46–51 follow Jer 25:13, but in a different order, an indication that the collection, and earlier some of its parts, originally circulated independently.

Not all of the material can be dated and certainly very little of it comes from Jeremiah himself. Probably only 46:3–12 and 47:1–7 can be attributed with certainty to him and can be dated around 605 B.C. Some of the material, such as the poems on Moab, are older than Jeremiah; some, such as passages concerning Babylon, date from the exilic period. The poems include borrowings from other prophets (Isaiah, Obadiah, Second Isaiah), and reworkings of original Jeremiah sayings (compare 50:41–43 with 6:22–24), but all of the material is probably to be dated not later than the middle of the sixth century B.C.

It is doubtful that any preachers will select texts from this collection, although great homileticians of the past have seized upon some of its portrayals to vivify the language of other sermons. For example, in a sermon on Nah 1:3, Charles Haddon Spurgeon utilized the metaphor of the sword of the Lord from Jer 47:6–7:

But God is slow to anger, and doth still stay His sword. Wrath said yesterday, "Unsheath thyself, O sword;" and the sword struggled to get free. Mercy put her hand upon the hilt, and said, "Be still!" "Unsheath thyself, O sword"! Again it struggled from its scabbard; Mercy put her hand on it, and said, "Back!"—and it rattled back again. Wrath stamped his foot, and said, "Awake, O sword, awake!" It struggled yet again, till half its blade was outdrawn; "Back, back!"—said Mercy, and with manly push she sent it rattling into its sheath: and there it sleeps still, for the Lord is "slow to anger, and plenteous in mercy" (*The Treasury of the Bible*, vol. 4, pp. 690–91).

Moreover, the theology contained in these oracles against the foreign nations is well worth pondering and preaching on.

First of all, the God portrayed in these oracles is absolute Lord of all nations—"the King, whose name is the Lord of hosts" (46:18; 48:15; 51:57), that is, who is Lord over all things in heaven and on earth, "the Holy One of Israel" (50:29). The world of these oracles is not governed finally by human beings, as we think our secular world is, and international relations are not solely dependent on politicians and economists and military leaders. Mighty Babylon is an instrument in the hand of God (51:7, 20–23), which he uses to work out his plan and purpose for the earth. But when Babylon sins against the Lord (50:14, 24) by proudly defying his will (50:29, 31) and plundering Israel beyond all reason (50:11; 51:34–37, 49), then God turns against her (51:25) and plans her deserved destruction (50:45; 51:12, 29).

Indeed, all nations are responsible to the Lord of hosts, according to these oracles, and they are judged because they have sinned against him. They have trusted in their own might and wealth (48:7; 49:4). They have taken advantage of God's people (49:1, 12) and derided Israel (48:27), thus magnifying themselves against God's purpose for his people (48:26, 42; 50:29, 31). They have been proud and insolent and haughty (48:29–30), thinking themselves invincible (49:4), and therefore they will be punished (46:21; 49:8). Their own cleverness and their false gods will be unable to save them from the wrath of the Lord (46:11, 15; 48:7, 13, 46; 50:2; 51:44, 47, 52).

Not only individuals and societies and churches are responsible to the God of the Bible, but also nations, and international relations are to be conducted in the light of his revealed will and purpose. That is the first message of these oracles, and considering the fate of Babylon, of Moab, of Edom, and the others, that is a sobering message indeed. But it is also a hopeful message, because it means that finally the earth's fate is not in the hands of sinful human beings, but in the hands of a loving and merciful God who, despite all their sin, finally wished a new covenant for his people. That is the hope for our dying world.

Second, though these oracles have sometimes been read as nothing more than the expressions of Israel's nationalistic hatred toward her enemies, it is doubtful that such an interpretation really does them justice. Israel takes no vengeance into her own hands here. All vengeance belongs to God. "Vengeance is mine. I will repay, says the Lord." And that bears two assurances—one, that there is a structure of divine justice at work in human history, which will right the wrong committed by proud and selfish human beings; second, that the only proper vengeance is that administered by a God who so loved the world that he gave his only Son for its sake. God's vengeance is ever the instrument of his loving purpose to make a kingdom of peace and righteousness on earth, and the proper response to such a God is therefore, "Though he slay me, yet will I trust him."

Should the preacher wish to set forth such theology in a sermon from these oracles, he or she would be wise to select one passage as a representative text, for example 51:1–10.

A Historical Appendix (52:1–34)

Apparently the final redactors of the Jeremiah material felt that it would be appropriate to end the book with a historical appendix, showing how the prophet's words were fulfilled in the fall of Jerusalem. They therefore used this account, which is found also in 2 Kings 24:18–25:30, but they omitted 2 Kings 25:22–26, because its content had already been more fully recorded in Jer 40:7–43:7.

The theology of the chapter is to be gleaned from a study of 2 Kings and should be interpreted in that context, although we might note that the hopeful notice of the release of the

Davidic heir, in vss. 31–34, accords well with Jeremiah's promise that God yet had a future for his exiled people.

Verses 28–30 are not found in Kings and evidently come from an unknown source. They give the numbers of those deported by Nebuchadnezzar from Judah in 598/7, 587/6, and 582/1 B.C. The numbers probably include only adult men, whose families therefore should be numbered with them (see 2 Kings 24:14, 16).

Bibliography

Achtemeier, Elizabeth, *Deuteronomy, Jeremiah* (Philadelphia: Fortress Press, 1978).

Bright, John, *A History of Israel* (3rd ed.; Philadelphia: Westminster Press, 1981).

Bright, John, *Jeremiah* (Anchor Bible 21; Garden City, NY: Doubleday and Co., Inc., 1965).

Carroll, Robert P., *Jeremiah, A Commentary* (Philadelphia: Westminster Press, 1986).

Holladay, William, "Jeremiah the Prophet," *The Interpreter's Dictionary of the Bible.* Supplementary Volume (Nashville: Abingdon Press, 1976), pp. 470–72.

Hyatt, J. Philip, *Jeremiah, Prophet of Courage and Hope* (Nashville: Abingdon Press, 1958).

Hyatt, J. Philip, "Introduction and Exegesis of Jeremiah," *The Interpreter's Bible.* Vol. 5 (Nashville: Abingdon Press, 1956).

Interpretation. A Journal of Bible and Theology. Richmond, Va: Union Theological Seminary. July 1955, April 1983 issues.

Leslie, E. A., *Jeremiah* (New York/Nashville: Abingdon Press, 1954).

Muilenburg, James, "Jeremiah the Prophet." *The Interpreter's Dictionary of the Bible.* Vol. 2 (Nashville: Abingdon Press, 1962), pp. 823–35.

Nicholson, E. W., *Jeremiah 1–25, 26–52* (Cambridge Bible Commentary on the New English Bible; New York: Cambridge University Press, 1973, 1975).

Perdue, Leo G., "Jeremiah in Modern Research: Approaches and Issues," *A Prophet to the Nations: Essays in Jeremiah Studies* (ed. by Leo G. Perdue and B. W. Kovacs; Winona Lake, Ind: Eisenbrauns, 1983), pp. 1–32.

Skinner, John, *Prophecy and Religion: Studies in the Life of Jeremiah.* (New York: Cambridge University Press, 1922).

Welch, A. C., *Jeremiah, His Time and Work* (London: Oxford University Press, 1928. Reprinted Oxford: Blackwells, 1951).